AMERICAN

MANUAL OF PHONOGRAPHY.

BEING A COMPLETE EXPOSITION

OF

PHONETIC SHORTHAND;

ESPECIALLY ADAPTED TO THE SCHOOL-ROOM, AND TO AFFORD THE FULLEST INSTRUCTION TO THOSE WHO HAVE NOT THE ASSISTANCE OF THE ORAL TEACHER.

BY ELIAS LONGLEY.

LONGLEY & BROTHER, PHONETIC PUBLISHERS,
WALNUT STREET, BETWEEN FOURTH & FIFTH,
CINCINNATI.
1854.

A. C. James, Stereotyper, Cincinnati, Ohio.

PREFACE.

In preparing this Manual of Phonetic Shorthand, the author has had but one leading object in view, namely: to afford a speedy means of acquiring a correct and practical knowledge of the much coveted art. The books that have heretofore been used have all answered a good purpose; but they have all, with one exception probably, been rendered comparatively obsolete by the introduction into the system of two or three important improvements. These are incorporated into the present work; and in all probability they will be the last changes that will be made for a considerable length of time, if not entirely the last.

In one important particular this treatise differs from all others that have been published; namely, the exercises to be written by the pupil are printed in phonetic spelling. By this arrangement two important advantages are gained: First; the learner will be made acquainted with the simplicity and utility of phonetic spelling as applied to printing, and will undoubtedly be so pleased with it as to become its ardent advocate; and a familiarity with it will also be of service to him hereafter, in enabling him to read with ease such phonetic books and papers as he may meet with elsewhere. Second; in writing his exercises the pupil will more readily transcribe the words into phonography. Learners are very apt to be troubled by trying to get as many letters into their phonographic word as the old spelling contains, and thus make blunders; but by writing from the words printed phonetically this difficulty will be avoided. And they can always tell whether their writing is correct, by referring to the tables where the shorthand characters are placed in juxtaposition with the printing characters.

Another leading feature is such an arrangement of the lessons that no word, or class of words, is required to be written until the principle has been explained by which they are written in their most approved forms. By this means, the student is not compelled to spend his time in learning how to write certain words, and then suffer the discouragement of having to drop and forget the forms thus learned, and familiarize himself with new and better ones. What is once learned in this book, remains a fixed fact with the pupil in all his after use of the system. There are hundreds of persons now, who, having studied Phonography through what was called the learner's style, have not yet been able to drop it and adopt the advanced and more practical style of writing; but they will have to do it before they can be recognized as good phonographic writers; and the unlearning of their present lengthy and awkward forms for words, added to the new forms they must learn, is fully equal to learning the system from the beginning.

In consequence of this progressive arrangement, the exercises to be written necessarily possess an imperfect style of composition. The past tenses of verbs, the comparatives and superlatives of adjectives, and, indeed, a large portion of the words in our language are written by contracted forms, which are introduced gradually through the book. And the words in each exercise being confined as much as possible to the illustration of the principle just introduced, renders necessary a resort to many circuitous expressions for the development of an idea; this harshness and quaintness, however, diminishes as successive lessons are mastered.

The review at the close of each chapter is a new feature, and will be of great assistance to the teacher, especially to the unexperienced, in questioning his class as to what they have gone over; it will also be useful to the private learner, filling the place, almost, of an oral teacher. The questions may be asked the class either collectively or individually; the latter is generally the better way. It would be well, as often as convenient, to have the pupils illustrate their answers on the black-board.

Immediately following the explanation of each new principle is an exercise for writing, which should be written before progressing further, while the manner in which the words are to be written are fresh in the mind. Then, at the close of each lesson, is an exercise for reading, embracing as much as possible, words illustrative of the preceding text. After this is a general writing exercise, embodying, beside the principles just presented, all that has previously been learned. This should be written by each pupil, during the interval between the meetings of the class; and at the next recitation, the pupils should exchange their manuscripts with each other, and then read, each a sentence in turn, from these written exercises. They might then be passed to the teacher for his correction.

As a substitute for this, the private learner is referred to the constitution of the American Phonetic Society, at the close of this book; which will inform him of a way in which he can secure the assistance of experienced phonographers, either for the correction of his exercises, or for mutual improvement, through the medium of phonographic correspondence.

The author would acknowledge his indebtedness to the *Phonographic Class-Book* of ANDREWS & BOYLE, the first text book of the system published in America, for many of his most appropriate illustrations; and to the *Phonographic Instructor*, by JAMES C. BOOTHE, the more recent work generally used, for numerous sentences, and, in a few cases, whole paragraphs of exercises for reading and writing.

Phonography is the invention of Mr. ISAAC PITMAN, of Bath, England. It is about fifteen years since he issued his first publication of the system; but only during the last ten years has it been taught, and but six since it was introduced into the United States. In the year 1843 a Phonetic Society was established in Great Britain, consisting of persons who had learned to write Phonography; its object was to promote the adoption of phonetic writing; it has gradually increased till it now numbers about four thousand members. A similar Society was established in the United States in 1849, which now numbers about one thousand members. But these Societies do not embrace a hundredth part of the persons who have learned to write the system. In 1850 a Phonetic Council of one hundred persons (fifty in Great Britain and fifty in America,) was elected by a popular vote of the phonographers of each country, for the purpose of uniting the efforts and skill of all in effecting some further improvements in the art, and in devising ways and means for promoting its general adoption. This Council, together with the assistance of both Phonetic Societies, have had the system under thorough revision for two years; and after so long and thorough experiments it is reasonable to believe that the system is as near perfection as it is possible for an art to approximate.

CONTENTS.

INTRODUCTION.

Within the last hundred years important changes have taken place in almost every department of industry. The mechanic no longer seeks the swiftly running stream to propel his machinery, but erects his mill or factory on ground the most convenient for labor or for market, and brings the elements into subjection for the performance of his drudgery; the stage-coach horse-power, for locomotion, is almost forgotten in consideration of the iron-boned steed hitched to the enormous wheeled palace; the sea-voyage of weary months is now performed pleasantly in as many weeks, by the application of steam to navigation; and the man of business no longer waits the rapid transmission of thought by such conveyance, but communicates through the length and breadth of our wide-spreading country with lightning speed.

Thus the genius of invention and improvement has been abroad in the land, and although for a long time she confined her skill to building steamboats and making railroads, constructing machinery and teaching the lightning how to talk, she has not altogether forgotten the world of intellect; and PHONOGRAPHY, her last, most promising and glorious boon, presents to the world an alphabet of letters so simple and facile that he who uses it may readily keep pace with the fastest speaker,—affording a system of writing as much superior to that of the old script alphabet, as railroads are to the ancient truck-wheeled wagon, or the electric telegraph to the post boy's plodding gait.

We do not wish to underrate the value of the present system of writing; it has been of great service in its time, having done much in the way of civilizing and enlightening the races of men. But the present state of things in the scientific world demands a change in the character of our written language. Science is a stern ruler; her laws encircle every art; and although for a long time they may remain undiscovered or not applied, yet as the world progresses in knowledge and learns wisdom from experience, it will cause them to be developed, and future generations will derive the advantages of conforming to them.—These facts have been illustrated in the various improvements to which we have alluded; and they are still to be expected in such departments as have not yet undergone the remodeling process of modern ingenuity. They take their turn in the great circle of progression; and it is our privilege now to demonstrate the laws that apply to the art of writing, as required at this stage of the world's history.

The spirit of our age demands two new features in the art of writing: First, *Speed in its execution;* second, *System in its orthography.* In treating of the first desideratum we shall briefly refer to the old romanic alphabet, and the habits of writing it requires. Like the ancient implements of industry and modes of labor, the alphabet of our fathers was constructed at a time when the ingenuity of man had not been brought into full play. The letters are complex, and the use of them cumbersome in the extreme. To illustrate: take the letter *l* for example; to make this letter, the fingers have to perform four inflections or movements, while it represents but a simple sound; in making the letter *m* seven inflections are required, while it, too, represents but one sound; and every letter of the old alphabet is thus complex, to a greater or less degree, although they are designed each to represent but a single sound.

Now, while there is this complexity in the art of writing, in spoken language the organs of speech perform but *one* movement in the enunciation of each letter; and hence the labor of the penman is four or five times as great as that of the speaker; while the latter is moving off freely, as on the wings of the wind, the former is trudging along at the snail's pace, weary and provoked at the contrast.

The object to be accomplished, therefore, is to present an alphabet each letter of which can be written by one inflection of the pen, so that the writer need no longer be four times distanced by the moderate speaker; and if the reader will follow us through this book, he will see that the system we are about to develop more than meets this requisition.

But a greater difficulty, if possible, than the mere substitution of a new alphabet, is to be overcome. The orthography employed in using the old alphabet is nearly as cumbrous as the formation of its letters; while its want of system makes it a study of many years to memorize the spelling of the fifty or eighty thousand words in our language.

Thus, take the sound of *a;* if we had nothing to do, in order to represent it in our common writing, but to write the one letter called *a*, the evil would be trifling compared with what it is. But we more frequently have to write two or three, and even four, letters to represent this one sound. It has, in fact, thirty-four different modes of representation, consisting of various combinations of nine different letters, a few only of which we have room to exhibit. Thus, *aa*, as in *Aa*ron, *ai*, as in p*ai*n, *aig*, as in campaign; *aigh*, as in str*aigh*t; *eighe*, as in w*eighe*d, &c. Now common sense, as well as the laws of science, suggests that the sound of *a* in each and all these should be written with the same letter. When this shall be done, more than *two thirds* of the labor of representing this sound will be saved; but by substituting a new letter that can be made with one movement of the pen instead of the four that *a* requires, and of the four times four that several of the above combinations require, *nine tenths* of this labor will be avoided. In writing the sound *a* in these five words, instead of making *fifty* inflections of the pen, we will have to make but *five!*

The sound of *e* is represented in *forty* different ways. Examples: *ea*, as in *ea*ch; *ea-ue*, as in l*eague*; *eye*, as in k*eye*d; *eig*, as in s*eig*nor; *eigh*, as in L*eigh*. We need not repeat that the sound of *e* in each of these words should be represented by the same letter; or that by substituting for the complex letter *e* a simple character that can be made with one motion of the pen, seven-eighths or nine-tenths of the labor in writing would be saved.—These are facts that are evident, after the illustrations are presented. And we might thus illustrate the unscientific mode of representing every word in our language, with equally formidable results. But we will only state the melancholy fact, that the various sounds employed in speaking the English language are each represented in from four to forty ways, and that in the large majority of cases two or more letters are required to do the service. And also, that there is no letter in the alphabet that uniformly represents the same sound. They are as changeable as the wind or the weather, and to the young learner exceedingly provoking. The consequence of this want of system is, in the language of a distinguished writer on the subject of education, that "reading is the most difficult of human attainments." And, as a further consequence, *one third* of the population of England are unable to read, and *one half* unable to write; while in the United States, although the proportion is considerably less, yet the number of illiterate persons is very great; and this wide-spread ignorance must continue until the rudiments of education are simplified. Such inconsistencies and mischievous errors as we have referred to, are not in harmony with the developments of order and science in most other branches of industry and art, and hence they must be superceeded by something truer and more expeditious.

THE PHONETIC PRINCIPLE.

The term *Phonetic* is derived from the Greek word *phone*, speech. A phonetic alphabet, therefore, is one which, referring solely to speech, derives all its laws from a consideration of the *elements of speech*. To illustrate what we mean by the phrase "elements of speech," we have but to ask the reader to adjust his lips to a round position and deliver the voice as he would commence to speak the words *ode, oak, own*. Now this same sound is heard in thousands of words in our language, and is what we call an element of speech. A similar element is heard in the commencement of the word *ooze*, and at the termination of the word *who*. In pronouncing the words *see, say, saw, so*, we hear, at the beginning of each of them, the same kind of a sound, namely a *hiss*, which is also an element of speech, for it frequently combines with other sounds to make words. By analyzing all the words in the English language, it has been found that it is constituted of but forty elementary sounds; or to be more precise, thirty-four simple sounds and six compound ones, formed by the close union of certain simple sounds which it is convenient to consider as distinct sounds. In speaking, therefore, our words consist simply in the utterance of one of these, or a combination of two or more of them; and in writing these words common sense would suggest that each element should be represented by a single letter, that should never stand for any other sound.

It is supposed the original Phœnician alphabet, from which our present alphabet is remotely derived, was phonetic; that is, it represented the elements of speech in such a manner that when the sounds of a word were heard the writer knew immediately what letters to use, and when he saw the letters he knew at once what sounds he was to utter. But when this alphabet was adopted by the Greeks and Romans, who used sounds unknown to the Phœnicians, many of the old letters were necessarily used to represent new sounds as well as old ones, so that there was no longer any very strict accordance between the sounds and letters of words. But when other European nations, including the English, adopted the *romanic* alphabet, and used it in very different ways, insomuch that no one could guess what sound could be attributed to any one letter, almost all trace of the phonetic nature of the alphabet was lost. And hence the deplorable state of English spelling and writing, as depicted in previous pages, which, in few words, is so bad that no one can tell the sound of an unknown word from its spelling, or the spelling of a new word from its sound.

Phonetic spelling, therefore, is no new thing, and the efforts of writing and spelling reformers is simply an attempt to place the representation of the English language on the same rational basis that the most classic of the ancient languages stood, and in addition thereto to afford the means of the most rapid writing that it is possible to attain. No further argument, therefore, should be required, in presenting a system so accordant with truth and utility.

PHONOTYPY.

The word Phonotypy, from the Greek *phone*, speech, and *tupos*, type, signifies the printing of language by types which represent the sounds heard in speaking; while Phonography, also from *phone* and another Greek word, *graphien*, to write, signifies to write by sound, or with characters that represent the sounds heard in speech. Although the latter is the art which this work is specially designed to explain, yet a knowledge of the former will materially aid in its acquisition; and as a sufficient acquaintance with it may be obtained in a few minutes' study, we shall here present a brief exposition of it.

The forty elementary and dipthongal sounds* that it has been found necessary to represent in a true orthography of the English language, are exhibited by the italic letters in the following words:—

*ee*l *a*le *a*rm *a*ll *oa*k *oo*ze,
*i*ll *e*ll *a*m *o*n *u*p w*oo*d;
*i*ce, *oi*l, *ow*l, m*u*te; *y*ea, *w*ay, *h*ay;
*p*ole, *b*owl, *t*oe, *d*oe, *ch*eer, *j*eer, *c*ame, *g*ame,
*f*ear, *v*eer, *th*igh, *th*y, *s*eal, *z*eal, *sh*all, vi*s*ion,
*r*are, *l*ull; *m*um, *n*un, si*ng*.

* Worcester's dictionary, and later writers on orthoepy, contend for a more minute analysis of sounds; thus, between the second and third vowels in the above scheme, they would represent the sound in *care* as differing from either that in *ale* or that in *arm;* and between the vowels in *arm* and *am* they would mark a different one in *fast, last,* &c.; also the vowel in *cur*, as distinct from that in *cut.* The dipthongs in *ice, oil, owl, mute*, they would represent by their elements, that is, in the case of *i*, they would represent it by the two letters that would represent the vowels in *arm* and *eel*; the dipthong in *oil*, by the vowels in *all* and *ill;* that in *owl* by the

Of course the old twenty-six letter alphabet was incompetent to give a character for each of these forty sounds. And in determining upon the introduction of new letters, two important considerations presented themselves to the mind, both grounded on the fact that the romanic style of spelling already existed in printed books, and flourishes wherever our language is spoken or read. First, that those who can already read romanic spelling should have very little difficulty in acquiring phonetic spelling; and secondly, that those who are taught to read phonetically should find that the greater part of the difficulties attendant on the acquirement of romanic reading were then overcome. In order to accomplish these two very important objects, it was necessary to use as many of the old romanic letters as possible in the senses which they most frequently have in the romanic spelling of English; and to make the new phonetic letters suggest the letters or combinations of letters which are most frequently employed to express their sounds romanically. The grand object was to make English reading easy—not merely in phonetic but also in romanic spelling, in order that the large number of books already printed should be still useful, or rather should be made useful to those to whom they are at present useless—the book-blind, those who cannot read. *This has been effected.* Not only is phonetic reading so easy to those who read romanically, that few find any difficulty in the matter at all, but those

vowels in *arm* and *ooze*; and that in *mute*, by the vowels in *ill* and *ooze*. The consonants *ch* and *j* they would dissolve into *t-sh* and *d-zh*. But the representation of such delicate shades of sounds is hardly practicable, at the present time, at least; it may be that under phonetic teaching the public ear will be trained so that a more nice representation will be advisable; though as regards the dipthongs and double consonants, it would be exceedingly distasteful to represent them by the letters of which they are composed, and we have no idea it will ever be done.

who have only learned to read phonetically are more than two-thirds on their way towards romanic reading.

Out of the twenty-six romanic letters, three, *c*, *q*, *x*, have been rejected. The fifteen consonants,

b d f h j l m n p r t v w y z

are used in their usual romanic sense; that is, in the sense which the English romanic reader would naturally expect them to have in any new word, as they are pronounced at the beginning of the romanic words,

*b*ed, *d*eed, *f*it, *h*ead, *j*est, *l*ull, *m*an, *n*un, *p*eep, *r*are, *t*oe, *v*ote, *w*oe, *y*es, *z*eal.

The five vowels, a, e, i, o, u, and the remaining three consonants, *k*, *g*, *s*, are to be pronounced as at the beginning of

*a*m, *e*gg, *i*n, *o*n, *u*p, *k*ite, *g*et, *s*up.

New letters have been invented for the sounds expressed by the italic letters in the under-written words in the following examples:

𐐀 𐐨	𐐁 𐐩	𐐂 𐐪	𐐃 𐐫	𐐄 𐐬	𐐅 𐐭	𐐋 𐐳	𐐌 𐐴	𐐦 𐑎
*ee*l	*a*ge	*a*rm	*a*ll	*o*ak	*oo*ze	f*oo*t	*i*ce	*oi*l

𐐍 𐐵	𐐧 𐑏	𐐕 𐐽	𐐛 𐑃	𐐜 𐑄	𐐟 𐑇	𐐠 𐑈	𐐤 𐑌
*ow*l	m*u*le	cat*ch*	*th*in	*th*ine	*sh*e	vi*s*ion	si*ng*

On the following page the whole alphabet is presented in a systematic arrangement; first, the vowels; second, the compound vowels; third, the liquids; fourth, the consonants. In this particular, unimportant though it may seem, the new alphabet is an improvement on the old—which is little more than a string of confusion—here a vowel and there a vowel, a consonant here and another there.

THE ENGLISH PHONETIC ALPHABET.

The letter written	The letter prntd	is *always* sounded as
Ɛ ɛ	Ɛ ɛ	*ee* in *ee*l
Ǝ ɘ	Ǝ ɘ	*a* .. *a*le
Ɑ ɑ	Ɑ ɑ	*a* .. *a*lms
Θ ɵ	Θ ɵ	*a* .. *a*ll
Ꞷ ω	Ꞷ ω	*o* .. *o*pe
Ɯ ɯ	Ɯ ɯ	*oo* .. f*oo*d
I i	I i	*i* .. *i*ll
E e	E e	*e* .. *e*ll
A a	A a	*a* .. *a*m
O o	O o	*o* .. *o*live
U u	U u	*u* .. *u*p
Ɯ ɯ	Ɯ ɯ	*oo* .. f*oo*t
Ɨ ɨ	Ɨ ɨ	*i* .. *i*sle
Ơ ơ	Ơ ơ	*oi* .. *oi*l
Ȣ ȣ	Ȣ ȣ	*ow* .. *ow*l
Ʉ ʉ	Ʉ ʉ	*u* .. m*u*le
Y y	Y y	*y* .. *y*ea
W w	W w	*w* .. *w*ay
H h	H h	*h* .. *h*ay

The letter written	The letter prntd	is *always* sounded as
P p	P p	*p* in *p*ole
B b	B b	*b* .. *b*owl
T t	T t	*t* .. *t*oe
D d	D d	*d* .. *d*oe
Ꞓ ꞓ	Ꞓ ꞓ	*ch* .. *ch*eer
J j	J j	*j* .. *j*eer
K k	K k	*c* .. *c*ame
G g	G g	*g* .. *g*ame
F f	F f	*f* .. *f*ear
V v	V v	*v* .. *v*eer
Ŧ ŧ	Ŧ ŧ	*th* .. *th*igh
Đ đ	Đ đ	*th* .. *th*y
S s	S s	*s* .. *s*eal
Z z	Z z	*z* .. *z*eal
Σ ʃ	Σ ʃ	*c* .. vi*c*ious
Ʒ ʒ	Ʒ ʒ	*s* .. vi*s*ion
R r	R r	*r* .. *r*a*r*
L l	L l	*l* .. *l*u*ll*
M m	M m	*m* .. *m*u*m*
N n	N n	*n* .. *n*u*n*
Ŋ ŋ	Ŋ ŋ	*ng* .. si*ng*

NOTE.—In the above table, in addition to the printing letters of the phonetic alphabet, are presented the longhand script characters. It will be observed that, as in the phonotypic scheme, the old letters are retained in their usual sense, and new ones introduced having resemblance to their corresponding printed letters, and of as easy formation as possible. This alphabet is used by Spelling Reformers, who are so in truth, in all cases where the phonetic shorthand could not be read by the person for whom the writing is done; for phonetic longhand may be read, with very little hesitation, by all who can read the old manuscript. And the writer in addition to the satisfaction of employing a scientific orthography, economizes twelve per cent of his paper and time, by dispensing with double letters.

PHONOGRAPHY.

Phonography being intended for the pen alone, and the principal object being rapidity of execution, with a moderate degree of legibility, considerable lisense is taken as regards strictly phonetic principles. It cannot be said of phonetic shorthand that "no sound must be represented by more than one sign," and that "no sign must represent more than one sound." The reverse of this statement is true in frequent instances; but not in such a way as materially to impair the scientific accuracy of the system. In point of utility there are great advantages derived from having two or three forms to represent certain sounds, and no serious disadvantage.

The simplest signs which it was possible to obtain for the phonographic alphabet, are, 1st, the *dot;* 2d, the *dash;* 3d, the *straight line;* 4th, the *curve.* The dots and dashes are used to represent the vowels; the straight lines and curves represent the consonants. The following diagrams exhibit the source from which the latter are derived, or rather the different positions to each other in which they are placed to represent different letters.

It will be observed that the straight line assumes four different positions, and the curved one eight; these are as many positions as can be recognized without danger of confusion; and these two simple characters can be written in these twelve positions so as to be just as distinct and legible as though this number of differently shaped letters were employed. Here now we have the means of representing twelve consonant sounds; but since in writing we can make either light or heavy marks, this number may be doubled by recognizing the same number of heavy lines and curves.

While it is found necessary to make each of the primitive characters heavy, in order to obtain a sufficient number, it is also found a useful and philosophical method of distinguishing between the natures of different sounds. Thus, eight of the sounds which these characters are to represent are mere *whispers*, produced by the transition of the organs of speech from one position to another, or by the simple contact of different parts of the mouth, without any vocal sound; and there are eight others made in the same manner, but have in addition a slightly roughened or *vocal* sound, which require a greater effort to produce them. To follow nature, therefore, and preserve a correspondence between signs and sounds, the light signs are made to represent the light or whispered sounds, and the heavy signs to represent the heavy sounds. Thus, both the *difference* between the sounds and their *resemblance* are at once represented. And it being so natural to represent a light sound by a light stroke, and a heavy sound by a heavy stroke, the phonographic pupil finds, after a little practice, that he makes the difference in the strokes without any thought about it. But the similarity of sound between the heavy and light strokes is so great that, if at any time the difference in the thickness of the lines is not clearly made, it will not seriously affect the legibility of the writing to the experienced phonographer. Thus, for example, if the word *Sinsinati* were written so as to be pronounced *Zinzinadi*, the reader could hardly mistake the intention of the writer.

The consonant sounds are classified as follows:—

1. *Abrupts:* These elements are produced by a total contact of the different organs of speech, abruptly interrupting the outward passage of the breath, or the voice. They are eight in number, and have the eight straight marks appropriated for their representation, as illustrated in the following table,—the italisized letters of the words indicating the sounds represented :

Whispered,	\ *p*ole,	| *t*oe,	/ *ch*air,	— *c*ame.
Spoken,	\ *b*owl,	| *d*oe,	/ *j*eer,	— *g*ame.

By a little observation in comparing the sound of *p* with that of *b*, in the words *pole* and *bowl*, the distinction of *whispered* and *spoken*, or light and heavy, will be appreciated. As far as articulation, or the contact of the organs of speech is concerned, the consonants *p* and *b* are identical; the sound of the former, however, is produced by the breath only, while the latter requires the assistance of the voice, which commences before the lips, the organs by which the articulation is produced, are disconnected. The same remarks apply to each of the other pairs of abrupts, as the reader will discover by speaking the illustrative words in connection.

2. *Continuants:* The organs of speech are in contact in the production of these elements, yet not so firmly as to totally obstruct the passage of breath, or voice; but the articulation may be continued any length of time. There are, also, eight of these elements—half of them whispered and half spoken. They may be illustrated as the abrupts were :

Whispered,	◡ *f*an,	(*th*in,	) *s*eal,	◞ *sh*un.
Spoken,	◡ *v*an,	(*th*en,	) *z*eal,	◞ vi*s*ion.

3. *Liquids:* These are *r* and *l*, and are called liquids because they readily run into or unite with other consonant sounds. They are not distinguished by any variation of sound, as the abrupts and continuants, and are represented by light curves; thus:

*r*ow, *l*ow.

4. *Nasals:* The sounds of *m*, *n*, and *ng*, are called nasals from the fact that the organs are brought in complete contact and the voice driven through the nose. The *m* and *n* are represented by the two remaining light curves, and *ng* by the heavy curve corresponding to *n*, as being nearly related to that sound; thus:

*m*u*m*, *n*u*n*, si*ng*.

5. *Ambigues:* These are *y*, *w* and *h*, and hold, as it were, a middle place between the vowels and consonants; their powers are more feeble than the other consonants, yet they must be recognized as belonging to that class of sounds, on account of their want of vocality.* They never occur in English except before a vowel; the *h* being simply a *breathing* upon the following vowel is often termed an *aspirate.* The following are their phonographic signs, and the words illustrating their powers:

*y*ea, *w*ay, *h*ay.

---

* Many persons imagine the powers of *y* and *w* to be *i* and *ɯ* or *u*; (see Phonotypic alphabet, p. 18,) and would spell words phonetically thus: *yet* iet; *yale* ial; yam iam; *week* ɯɛc or uɛc, *wall* ɯol, *worm* ɯurm; &c. We admit this representation is an approximation to the true one; but these vowels have too great powers for the weak whispers to be represented, as will be seen if we take words in which the same vowel would follow; take *yeast* iɛst, *year* iɛr, and *wound* ɯɯnd, or *wool* uul; and it will readily be seen that they do not afford just the pronunciation we want; and beside, this representation would make monosyllables into words of two syllables, because every vowel in a word requires a distinct syllabic pronunciation.

VOWEL ARRANGEMENT:—In order to represent the twelve vowel sounds by the two signs, a dot and a dash, a scheme similar to that of representing musical sounds by the round note is resorted to. As the vowels rarely occur except in combination with a consonant, they are indicated by the position in which the dot or dash is placed to the consonant stroke; thus, a dot placed at the beginning of a consonant represents the vowel *ε* (ee,) at the middle, *a* (age,) at the end, *q* (ah;) the dash at the beginning is *e* (awe,) at the middle, *o* (owe,) at the end, *u* (oo.) The remaining six vowels are short or brief, as compared with the foregoing six, and are appropriately represented by the dot and dash in the same manner, but made *lighter;* and all that has been said in regard to light and heavy consonants applies to the vowels. In the following illustration the vowel signs are placed to a dotted line merely to indicate the position of the dot and dash; it is no part of the vowel. The italic letters in the accompanying words suggest the vowel sounds:

*ee*l, *a*le, *a*rm, *a*ll, *o*ak, *oo*ze.

*i*ll, *e*ll, *a*m, *o*n, *u*p, w*oo*d.

Diphthongs: These being compound sounds, and all the simple characters being otherwise disposed of, they are represented by complex signs. They will be understood by the following illustration:

*i*sle, *oi*l, *ow*l.

Tripthongs: These result from the union of *w* with each of the above diphthongs, which are more convenient to represent by single characters than otherwise; thus:

*wi*ne, q*uoi*t, *wou*nd.

On the following page the whole alphabet is presented in a tabular form.

PHONOGRAPHIC ALPHABET.

CONSONANTS.

Abrupts.

Sign	Letter	Example
╲	p	*p*ost
╲	b	*b*oast
|	t	*t*ip
|	d	*d*ip
╱	ç	*ch*est
╱	j	*j*est
—	k	*k*ite
—	g	*g*et

Continuants.

Sign	Letter	Example
	f	*f*at
	v	*v*at
(	ŧ	*th*igh
(	đ	*th*y
)	s	*s*eal
)	z	*z*eal
╱	ʃ	*sh*e
)	ʒ	vi*s*ion

Liquids.

Sign	Letter	Example
	r	*r*ay
	l	*l*ay

Nasals.

Sign	Letter	Example
	m	*m*et
	n	*n*et
	ŋ	si*ng*

Ambigues.

Sign	Letter	Example
	y	*y*ea
	w	*w*ay
	h	*h*ay

VOWELS.

Long.

Letter	Example
ε	*ee*l
a	*a*le
ɑ	*a*rm
ɵ	*aw*ed
o	*o*pe
ɯ	f*oo*l

Short.

Letter	Example
i	*i*ll
e	*e*ll
a	*a*m
o	*o*dd
u	*u*p
ɯ	f*u*ll

Dipthongs.

Letter	Example
ị	*i*sle
ơ	*oi*l
ɤ	*ow*l

Tripthongs.

Letter	Example
wị	*wi*nd
wơ	qu*oi*t
wɤ	w*ou*nd

ADDITIONAL.—For the satisfaction of those who wish to represent a more critical pronunciation than the above scheme enables them to do, the following additions are suggested:

For the vowel in *care*, ꞌ¦ written thus, ⌐╲

For the vowel in *ask*, ꞌ¦ written thus, ꞌ)

For the close diphthong in *mute*, ,¦ written thus, ⌐,|

MANUAL OF PHONOGRAPHY.

LESSON I.

ON WRITING AND VOCALIZING THE SIMPLE CONSONANTS.

If the learner of Phonography has attentively read the preceding Introduction, and obtained a clear idea of the phonetic principle, he will find no difficulty in mastering the course of lessons which follows. The following arrangement of the consonant phonographs affords a kind of picture to the student which will enable him to fix in his mind the power of each letter by the position it has in the table. It will be as important to learn the phonotypic as the shorthand letters, because the exercises to be written are printed in phonotypy, as a means of greatly assisting the pupil in writing his lessons.

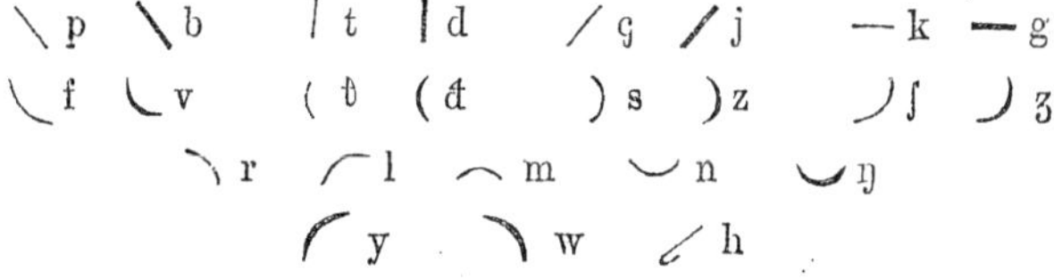

1. The perpendicular and inclined consonants are written from the top downward; the horizontal ones are written from left to right.

2. Exceptions.—The ⌒ *l*, when the only consonant in a word, is always written upward; at other times it may be written either upward or downward, as is most convenient. *ʃ* is always written downward when the only consonant in a word, and either downward or upward at other times. ⁄ is written upward.

3. Ruled paper should be used; and, for the first few exercises, until the pupil becomes familiar with the characters, a pencil should be employed in preference to a pen, after which either a pen or pencil may be used,—either of which should be held loosely between the first and second fingers and the thumb, as when used for drawing. The beginner generally experiences some difficulty, unless he has been accustomed to back-hand writing, in making the strokes from left to right; and is apt to imagine that he shall never be able to strike \ with the same ease with which he can execute / This difficulty is, however, entirely the result of habit in writing otherwise; and after a very short practice he will find that the muscles acquire complete facility in this and all the other movements required in Phonography.

4. The consonants should be written about the size of those given in these pages; and particular attention should, at first, be observed in writing the curved thick letters, making them thick in the middle only, and tapering to a light line toward each extremity. The inclined strokes should be written at an inclination of 45 degrees, or midway between the horizontal and vertical. Commence the strokes so that when of the proper length they will rest on the line of writing.

Let the pupil now take his pen or pencil, and go through the list of consonants, writing them as in the preceding table, speaking at the same time the power of the letter; and observing, also, the light and heavy character of the signs, and their proper length.

5. In order to establish some mode of writing the vowels, the point where the consonant stroke is commenced is called the *first* place, the middle of the stroke its *second* place, and where it ends, the *third* place.

VOWEL SCHEME.

long.	short.	long.	short.
ε	i	θ	o
a	e	ω	u
q	a	ɯ	ɯ

6. The proper sounds of these dots and dashes, in their several positions, should be well memorized. They may be designated thus:—*ε* is the first place heavy dot; *a* is the second place heavy dot; *q* is the third place heavy dot; *θ* is the first place heavy dash; *ω* is the second place heavy dash; *ɯ* is the third place heavy dash; *i* is the first place light dot, &c.; *o* is the first place light dash, &c.

7. In order to insure getting the dots and dashes in their proper positions, the consonant phonographs, whether one or many, are always written first; thus, *tk*, *nd*, *ltl*, *gg*. This gives what is called the *skeleton* of the word, and the vowels are jotted in afterward, similar to dotting the *i*s and crossing the *t*s in the longhand.[7]

8. In vocalizing the consonants, that is, in placing the vowels to them, they should be written near the strokes, but not so that they will join; the dashes should be written at right angles with the consonants; thus, *εv*, *pa*, *pθ*, *tɯ*, *fω*, *gω*, *nω*.

---

7. This may seem like a tedious process, and is, to the learner, for sometime; but, as he becomes accustomed to it, it will be done very readily; and as he becomes familiar with the appearance of the writing the necessity for vocalizing will cease, to a considerable extent, and only the accented, or distinguishing vowels will need to be inserted ;—the consonant outlines of words, assisted by the sense of the sentence, generally indicating the true words; just as the frame work of a building, or the skeleton of an animal, suggests to the mind at once what the structure would be if all its parts were

9. As in covering a page with writing we proceed from left to right, and from the upper to the lower line, so, in writing the dots and dashes, if we wish the vowel to read first we write it before the consonant, if perpendicular or inclined, (the inclined strokes, whether straight or curved, being treated as though they were perpendicular,) and above, if horizontal; thus, *et,* *ap,* *ar,* *am,* *ok,* if we wish it to read after the consonant, we write it after or below the stroke; thus, *bo,* *ha,* *le,* *fu,* *mq,* *ne.*

10. Words containing only horizontal consonants, if the accented vowels be first place, are written about the height of a vertical stroke above the line; as *me,* *ke;* if the vowels be second or third place, they are written on the line; as, *ga,* *mo.* EXCEPTIONS: *him* is written on the line, to prevent confounding it (should the vowels be omitted,) with the word *me;* and *eni* is written above the line, to obviate its being read *no.*

MARKS OF PUNCTUATION: × period, ‡ colon, interogation, wonder, grief, laughter, ( ) parenthesis; the comma and semi-colon may be written as in common manuscript.

An emphatic word or sentence is indicated by a waved line being drawn beneath it, thus: ; if it is desired to indicate that a word should commence with a capital letter, it is shown by two parallel dashes being written directly under it: thus, =

REVIEW.—(1.) Which of the consonant phonographs are written downwards? How are the horizontal ones written? What are they? (2.) Are there any exceptions to these general rules? and what are they? (3.) How are the sounds of the vowels designated? Speak the three heavy dot vowels. The three heavy dash vowels. The three light dot. The light dash. (6.) Designate the vowel *a—i—q—e,* &c., &c. (7.) What is the order in writing the consonants and vowels of a word? (8.) How are the vowels written to the consonants? (9.) In what directions are the letters in a phonographic word read? To which class do the inclined strokes belong? (10.) How are words containing only horizontal strokes written? What are the exceptions?

READING EXERCISE I.

The following exercises should be read over frequently, till the learner acquires the correct sounds of the vowels and their consecutive order. They will, at the same time, become familiar with many of the consonants.

*ee*l *a*le *a*rm *a*ll *o*pe f*oo*l

*i*ll *e*ll *a*m *o*n *u*p f*u*ll

READING EXERCISE II.

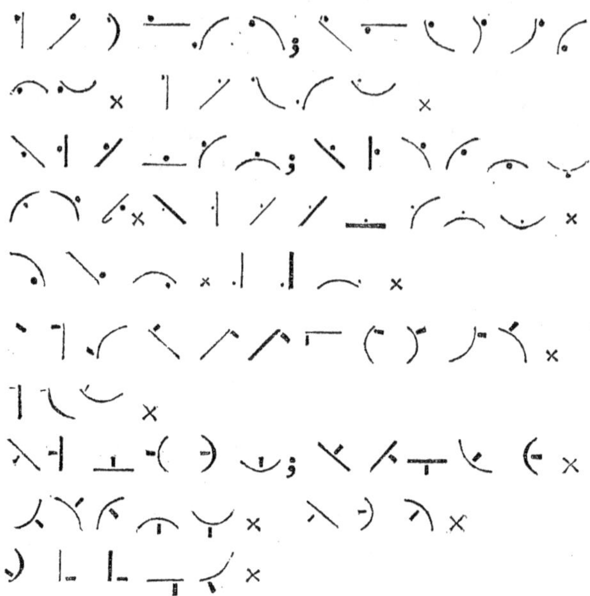

11. In vocalizing the consonants of a word, the first thing to be done is to ascertain whether the first vowel to be written is a dot sign or a dash sign; and, secondly, whether it is a long sound or a short sound; and lastly, what place to the consonant it should occupy. If the learner's memory is not good, or his perception quick, so that he can decide these points readily, a good plan for arriving at the results is to commence at the beginning of the scale of vowels and speak them thus, *ε i, ɑ, e, q a,*

(observing that thus far the signs are dots, heavy and light, and that the remainder are dashes,) *ɵ o, ɷ u, ɯ u,* till he arrives at the one he wishes to write ; just as the learner of music, when he cannot strike the proper sound of a note, commences at *do* and runs up the scale till he obtains the proper sound.

NOTE.—For the purpose of assisting the learner until he becomes familiar with phonetic printing, a few of the first exercises for writing will be printed in both modes of spelling.

WRITING EXERCISE I.

Ape, eat, eight, age, ache, eve, ease, ale, ear, air, aim.
Ɛp, ɛt, at, aj, ak, ɛv, ɛz, al, ɛr, ar, am.

Ebb, it, ate, add, itch, edge, egg, if, ill, am.
Eb, it, et, ad, iç, ej, eg, if, il, am.

Ope, ought, ode, oak, off, oath, owes, ooze, all, or, own.
ɷp, ɵt, ɷd, ɷk, ɵf, ɷθ, ɷz, ɯz, ɵl, ɵr, ɷn.

Up, odd, of, us, err, on.
Up, od, ov, us, ur, on.

Pea, pay, pa, tea, day, jay, key, gay, fee, they, see,
Pɛ, pa, pɑ, tɛ, da, ja, kɛ, ga, fɛ, đa, sɛ.

say, she, ray, lee, me, may, ma, nay, yea, way, hay.
sa, ʃɛ, ra, lɛ, mɛ, ma, mɑ, na, ya, wa, ha.

Paw, beau, toe, do, jaw, caw, coo, go, thaw, though,
Pɵ, bɷ, tɷ, dɯ, jɵ, kɵ, kɯ, gɷ, θɵ, đɷ,

saw, sow, show, law, low, raw, rue, know, woe, hoe.
sɵ, sɷ, ʃɷ, lɵ, lɷ, rɵ, rɯ, nɷ, wɷ, hɷ.

LESSON II.

THE DIPHTHONGS — DOT *H* — COMBINED CONSONANTS.

i. *ɒ*. *ȣ*.

12. These diphthong characters occupy but two places, the beginning and end of a consonant. When written in the first place, with the point downward, the angle represents the first sound in *isle;* with the point upward, in the same place, the first sound in *oil;* with the point upward, and in the third place, the first sound in *our*. The characters should be written without lifting the pen, and placed in a perpendicular position to the inclined and horizontal strokes as well as to the vertical; thus, *pi*, *đi*, *mi*, *bɒ*, *kɒ*, *ȣr*, *nȣ*.

WRITING EXERCISE II.

Bi, ti, fi, vi, đi, si, ʃi, li, ri, mi, ni; is,
By, tie, fie, vie, thy, sigh, shy, lie, rye, my, nigh; ice,

iz, il, ir, isi. Bɒ, tɒ, jɒ, kɒ; ɒl, anɒ. Bȣ,
eyes, aisle, ire, icy. Boy, toy, joy, coy; oil, annoy. Bow,

dȣ, kȣ, vȣ, sȣ, rȣ, alȣ, nȣ; ȣt, ȣr, ȣl.
dow, cow, vow, sow, row, allow, now; out, our, owl.

---

13. Dot H.—Since the aspirate never occurs in English except before a vowel, a briefer mode of representing it than the long sign is generally employed, namely, a light dot placed immediately before the vowel; it should be written to the left of the *dot* vowels that belong to a vertical or inclined stroke, and above those belonging to horizontals; and above the *dash* vowels of the former, and to the left of those of the latter; thus, *hit*, *hiɡ*, *hem*, *hod*, *hur* *hom*.

Although this *h* is the same in shape as the light dot vowels, it need never lead to any mistake, from the fact that no dot vowel ever occurs immediately before another dot vowel.

READING EXERCISE III.

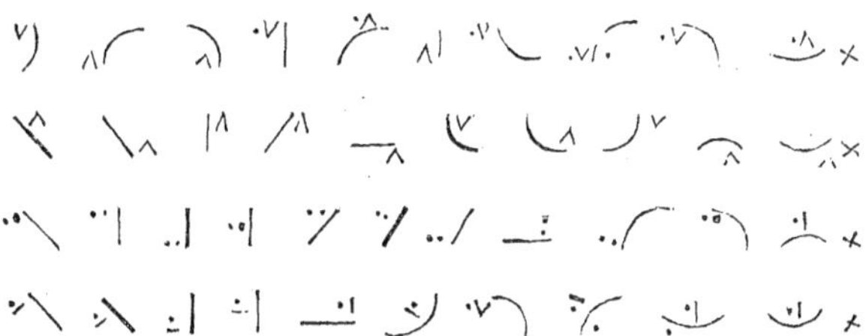

WRITING EXERCISE III.

Hɛp, hɑt, hɛd, hɛv, hɛt hɛl, hɑl, hɛr, hɑr;
Heap, hate, heed, heave, heat, heal, hail, hear, hair;

hat, hed, hiç, hej, haʃ, hil, him, ham, haŋ.
hat, head, hitch, hedge, hash, hill, him, ham, hang.

Hɷp, hɯp, hɷd, hɵk, hɷl, hɷm; hop, hub, hot,
Hope, hoop, hood, hawk, hole, home; hop, hub, hot,

hɯd, hog, hug, hur, hum, huŋ; hapi, hevi, hɵti,
hood, hog, hug, her, hum, hung; happy, heavy, haughty,

hɷli, huni.
holy, honey.

Hįt, hįv, hįr, hįli; hʊl.
Height, hive, hire, highly; howl.

Hɛ mɑ gɷ hɷm nʊ. Σɷ nɷ hɵti ɑr.
He may go home now. Show no haughty air.

COMBINED CONSONANTS.

14. In commencing to write a word, the first thing the learner has to do is to pronounce it slowly, and ascertain what are the elementary sounds of which it is composed, and then write the consonant signs, as heretofore directed. When the first consonant to be written requires a downward stroke, it is commenced its length above the line of writing and struck to the line, and if a downward stroke follow, it is carried on below the line; thus, *pt*, *dp*; if the first consonant be a horizontal stroke, and a down-stroke follow, it is written above the line and the second one carried to it; thus, *kd*, *ng*; but if an up-stroke sign follow the horizontal, the latter should be written on the line; thus, *ml*, *kl*.

15. In reading the consonants in a word, they must of course be uttered in the order in which they were written; thus, for example, in reading the must be read first, because it is evident it was written first, as the writer could not have begun at the angle and written the / and then gone back and written the , without violating the rule requiring the skeleton of a word to be written before lifting the pen; and he could not have begun at the bottom of the /, and written it upwards, and then the backwards, without violating the two rules, that *g* is to be written downwards and *n* from left to right.

It sometimes happens that a consonant which seems to be farther along than another in the line of writing, must be read first; as ; but from the fact that / is always to be written downward, we know the letters are to be read *jl* and not *lj*. By a little observation of this kind the learner will soon see at a glance, and without thought, how any word is to be read.

16. In vocalizing two or more consonants it is very important to keep the vowel signs away from the angles or places where the consonants join, especially from the inside of angles, as in such positions it is impossible to tell to which stroke they belong; thus, it cannot be told whether is the word *bɛm* or *bɑm*.

17. After the shape of a vowel, and the place it should occupy, are determined, the following rules, in addition to those for vocalizing single consonants, are to be observed:

First. When a first place vowel, or diphthong, comes between two consonants it is placed immediately after the first; as *kɛp*, *rɛm*, *kit*.

Second. A second place vowel, if it be long, is also written after the first consonant; as *gat*, *dɷm*; but if short, it is written before the second; as *get*, *dum*; by which arrangement we are enabled to determine the sound of the middle place vowel by position as well as by the size of the dot or dash.

Third. Third place vowels are written before the second consonant; as *bɑm*, *but*, *dst*.

Fourth. If two vowels come between two consonants, the first one spoken is written to the first stroke, and the next one to the second; thus, *pɷem*, *paliat*.

Some deviations from these rules occur in contracted forms of writing; but their general observance renders the manuscript more legible than it could otherwise be.

18. If two vowels precede the first consonant in a word, the first is written farther from the consonant than the second; thus, *iɷta*; if it terminate with two, the last is written farther from the consonant sign; as, *idɛa*.

19. When the diphthong ᵛ commences a word it is customary to go on writing the following consonant without lifting the pen, as in the word *idea*, just given, *item*, &c.; and the practice is extended, without any danger of ambiguity, and with much saving of time, to the connection of the pronoun *I* with the following word; as, *i bɛlev*, *i fɛr*. In this latter case the writing is entirely legible, even if the first prong of the angle is omitted, which is often done, for the sake of brevity.

20. In reading words of two or more consonants, it must be observed that each stroke, and the vowel-sign or signs placed to it, must be read precisely as they would be if they stood unconnected with other consonant strokes; thus, read in this way would be considered thus: *po-li-si*; , if analyzed thus: would reveal the word *rɛaliti*. This process will be necessary till the learner can read words from their general appearance.

READING EXERCISE IV.

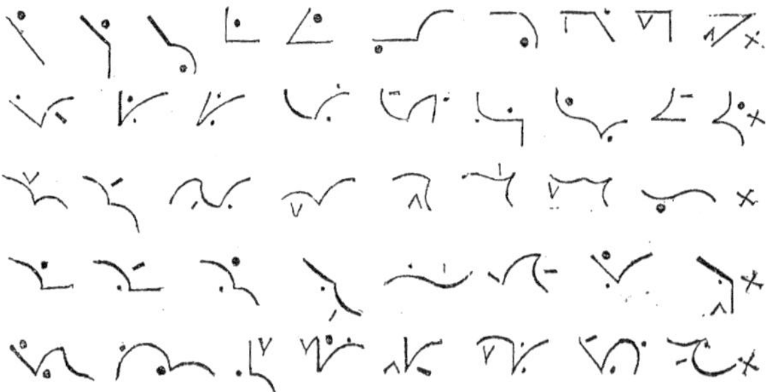

REVIEW.—(12.) How many diphthongs are there? Speak the first, and describe its sign; the second; the third. How are they to be written? (13.) What is the second form of the aspirate? How should it be placed to the dot vowels?—the dash vowels? (14.) How are the consonant signs adjusted to the line of writing? (15.) What is the order of reading words having two or more consonants? (16.) In vocalizing what is very important? (17.) What is the rule for writing first-place vowels that come between two consonants?—the rule for second-place vowels?—for third place vowels? If two vowels occur between two consonants, how are they to be written? (18.) If two vowels begin or terminate a word, how are they to be written? (19.) What peculiarity is practiced in writing the diphthong *I*? (20.) What is the rule for reading a word having two or more consonants and accompanying vowels?

WRITING EXERCISE IV.

Bɛt, bɑk, bɑr, pɛç, bqm, pɑd, pɑl, pqm, tɛm, dɑm, tqr, dɛd, dɑt, çɛp, çɑr, çɛr, çɛf, kɛp, gɑt, kɛl, gɑl, kɑm, kɑk, ʃɑm, qrk, qrm, hqrp, lɛp, lɑt, lqf, nɑv, nɑm, awɑk, awɑr.

Bit, pet, pad, piç, beg, bag, pil, del, fil, vali, ril, rim, rali, lip, lej, liv, maç, meʃ, maʃ, mil, milk, ahed.

Bөt, pωp, bɯt, tөt, dωr, tɯl, çөk, jωk, kөl, kωl, kɯl, gөdi, fөl, fөrm, vωt, fɯd, rωg, rɯm, lωf, mөl, mɯv, nөti, awωk.

Pot, bug, bɯk, bodi, dot, doj, dug, kɯk, foli, fɯli, ʃok, ʃɯk, rok, rug, rɯk, lok, luk, lɯk, mok, mug, muʃ, nok, nuj, nɯk.

Pj̧l, abj̧d, bөl, çj̧d, fɤl, çj̧m, abɤt, mj̧l, dɛkơ, dɛlj̧t, avɤd, alɤd, enjơ, bơlur, fj̧lur.

Get mɛ mj̧ bɯk. Put awɑ mj̧ dul nj̧f. Fil mj̧ kup fɯl. Fөrm nω bad habit in bơhɯd; it mɑ efect đj̧ helθ—đj̧ hωp in ɑj. Hɛ mɑ bɛ fөlti—nɑ, gilti. Foli mɑ fɑl at leŋθ.

LESSON III.

THE UP-STROKES *R*, *S* AND *L*—VOWEL WORD-SIGNS.

21. In order to prevent words from running too far below the line for convenience or beauty, and to afford a variety of skeleton outlines, by which different words having the same consonant sounds may be written differently, and thus be distinguished without being vocalized, provision is made for representing several of the consonant sounds by both upward and downward strokes. This provision also makes the writing more easy of execution, since these up-strokes are all in the inclination of the line of writing, from left to right. The letters thus represented are *ſ*, *l*, and *r*; the latter of which, only, requires a different character.

22. The second sign for *r* is a straight line struck upward at an angle of thirty degrees; thus, ⁄ Though this character is specially available in writing words requiring two or more consonants, yet it is frequently used alone; as ⁄ *ri*, and more frequently when terminating with a circle or hook, (Lessons IV, VI,) when it is less likely to be confounded with *ç*, written downward and of nearly the same inclination; in neither case, however, is there any difficulty experienced by the adept, since the sense of the preceding words nearly always suggests what the following word is.

23. When written in connection with other consonants, there is never any ambiguity, since it can be seen at a glance whether the stroke is written upward or downward; thus, *tr*, *tç*, *rt*. So that while the rule is that

ɡ shall be written at an angle of sixty degrees, and *r* at an angle of thirty degrees, they may both be written at the same inclination, except when either is the only consonant in a word; and except, also, when one of them immediately follows the other, as , in which case necessity compels one to be written at a different inclination from the other.

24. The rule that the *beginning* of a consonant stroke is where the first-place vowel is written, and the *termination* of a stroke the third-place, must be observed in vocalizing this up-stroke *r*; thus, *riɡ*, *rip*, *ɡariti*.

25. The following rules in regard to the use of the two forms of *r*, will guide the learner to the best forms of words:

First. The up-stroke should be used when the following consonant is to be written downward, as in the examples above. (24.)

Second. When *r* is the initial letter of a word, and is followed by the *s*-circle, *n*-hook, (see Lessons IV and VIII,) *k*, *g*, *ʃ*, *l*, or another *r*, the up-stroke is employed; as *rog*, *raʃ*, *rol*, *rar*. But if a vowel precede *r* as the first consonant, the down-stroke is employed; as, *ark*, *ɛriʃ*, *urli*, *erur*.

Third. Whenever preceded by *v*, *ŧ*, or *m*, the upward *r* is employed; as *ver*, *mir*.

Fourth. Whenever followed by *n* or *ŋ*, the up-stroke is employed; as *rani*, *roŋ*.

Fifth. When *r* is the final *stroke* consonant in a word, *and followed by a vowel*, the *up-stroke* is to be used, as in the words *beri*, *kari*; but if no vowel follow, the down-stroke is employed; as *pur*, *kar*.

Sixth. When one *r* follows another, except at the beginning of a word when preceded by a vowel (as in *erur*,) they are both written upward; as *rɛriti*, *kariur*.

Seventh. When followed by *m*, the down-stroke is always used; as *rum*, *gɑrm*.

READING EXERCISE V.

WRITING EXERCISE V.

Rɛpɛl, rɛtʝr, rɛdɛm, redi, ratifʝ, rɛvʝl, ravej, pɑrti, pɛriud, dɛrʝd, arʝv, aranj, urj, urθ; raʃ, rak, riketi. Borɷ, feri, ʝvɷri, θɛɷri, kari, memɷri, rɷtari, θurɷli, mɛr, dɛmur, admʝr. Randum, raŋk, rɛanimat, adɷriŋ. Borɷur, bɷrur, bariur, infɛriur, narɷur, kuriur, mirur, dɛrur, ʃɛrur, karɛr. Rɛm, rʝm, remedi, rɛmɯv, rɯminat, lɑrk, rɛfɵrm.

---

26. *L* and *ʃ* may be written upward or downward without any change of form; and in vocalizing, or reading, *the direction in which they were made*, as in the case of the up-stroke *r*, will be known by their connection with other consonant signs; as *loŋ*, *lɛv*, *ʃop*, *ʃol*.

27. The following rules will guide, as near as possible, to the most approved use of *l*.

First. When *l* is the initial letter of a word, and followed by *k*, *g*, or *m*, the up-stroke *l* is employed; as *lik*, *leg*, *lim*. But if a vowel precede, the down-stroke is used, as *alik*, *helm*. When other consonants follow *lk*, *lg*, *lm*, the *l* may be written either upward or downward.

Second. Immediately before or after *n* and *ŋ*, the down-stroke is employed; as *nal*, *liŋk*. If a down-stroke letter is to follow *l* after *n*, the up-stroke *l* must be employed; as *analoji*, *anihilat*.

Third. When *l* is the final stroke consonant in a word, and is preceded by *f*, *v*, or upward *r*, it is written downward; as *fel*, *revil*, *rul*, *moral*. But if a vowel follows, the up-stroke is used; as *foli*, *reli*.

Fourth. After *n* and *ŋ*, a final *l* is always written downward, even though followed by a vowel, as *lonli*, *kiŋli*.

Fifth. Final *l*, following all other consonants but *f*, *v*, up-stroke *r*, *n* and *ŋ*, is written upward, whether a vowel follows or not; as *pel*, *kul*, *mal*.

28. *Σ* is usually written downward; before *l*, however, and after *f* and *v*, it is always written upward; as *self*, *fiʃ*, *laviʃ*.

NOTE.—Many of the foregoing rules in regard to writing *r* and *l* upward or downward, are designed to secure consonant outlines that will be more legible, when not vocalized, than if written differently. Thus, when either up-stroke *r* or *l* is used at the commencement of a word, we know it does not commence with a vowel; if up-stroke *r* terminate a word, we know a vowel follows; and the same if up-stroke *l* after *f*, *v* and upward *r* terminate a word; and hence the chances of misreading the word are lessened.

The observance of the other rules will produce uniformity of writing, and thus ensure greater fluency in reading.

READING EXERCISE VI.

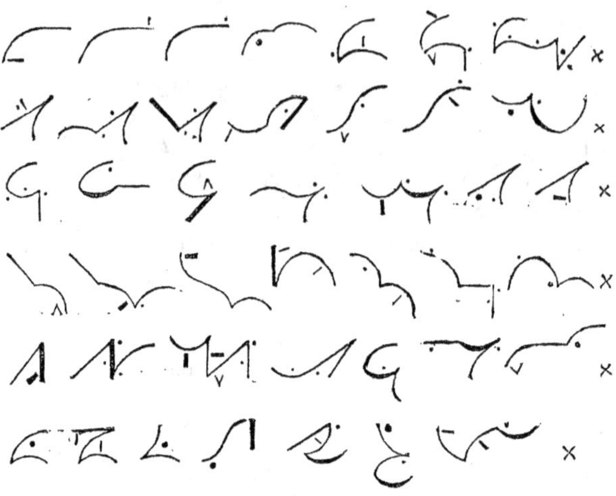

WRITING EXERCISE VI.

Lɛk, log, lɷm, legasi; alkalʝ, ɵlmanak. Lɑnɡ, laŋk, leŋθ, leŋθili, linsi, lunɡ, fɛliŋ; anul, ɷnli, kanal; analitik, lonjeviti, enlɑrj; fʝl, fɯl, vʝl, unfɐliŋ, rɛvɛl, unvɐl. Rɛl, rɛal, relm, ɷral, karul, barel, peril. Felɷ, fɯli, vali, rali, rɛali, rɛaliti; ɷnli, mɛnli, fɛliŋli, luviŋli; ʃʝli, ʃel, ʃalɷ; daʃ, nɐviʃ, efiʃensi, dɛfiʃensi; [down-stroke ʃ,] reliʃ, fɯliʃ, publiʃ, poliʃ, aboliʃ, raʃli.

WORD-SIGNS.

29. By a *word-sign* is meant the use of a single character of the alphabet to represent an entire word. This scheme is resorted to that the penman may attain greater speed in writing; and those words are chosen thus to be

represented, which occur the most frequently in composition; twenty-five of them actually constituting one-fourth of any given chapter or discourse, and one hundred of them amounting to almost half. The signs are so chosen as to suggest, generally, the words they represent. They should be memorized by copying the table once or twice.

30. TABLE OF VOWEL WORD-SIGNS.

the	all	already	or
a	two	oh, owe	who
	of		on
an, and	to	but	should
DIPHTHONGS,	*I*,	*how*.	

The first line of signs, since they are first-place vowels, are to be written at the height of a stroke above the line of writing; those in the second line, consisting of second and third-place signs, are to be written on the line. The second-place vowels are thus brought down because three places cannot be distinguished without a consonant stroke; but no confusion arises from it, since, when the second-place sign is thus transferred, the third-place sign is not used as a word-sign, and when the third is used the second is not. The third and fourth lines of the table have the same relation to each other as the first and second.

31. *The* is a word-sign that often follows immediately after most of the others, and in order to avoid lifting the pen to write each separately, it is joined to the preceding sign in the shape of a light tick; thus, *of the*, *on the*, *to the*.

READING EXERCISE VII.

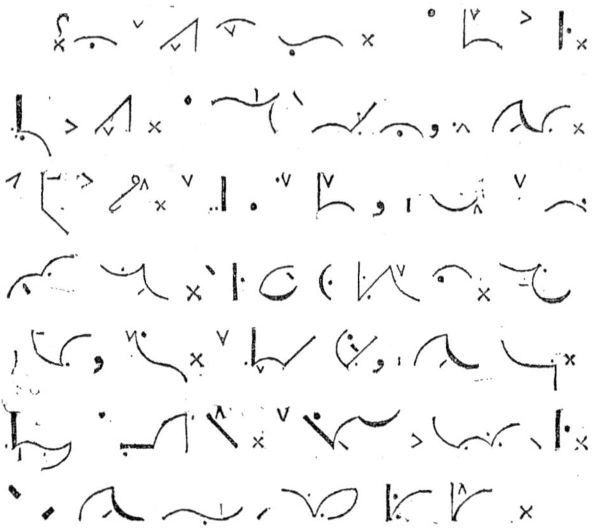

WRITING EXERCISE VII.

Ȼariti tarieθ loŋ; hı̧deθ muç roŋ; çeriʃeθ nω il; apεreθ hωlli luvli amuŋ us. Ꞇε urθ and ꞇε ɑr. Ɛɪ lı̧vli and hapi, but gidi, bơ. Ŧ ω nuθiŋ. Ꞇε hεt ov ꞇε fı̧r. Gω tɯ ꞇε dωr. Hε mɑ rı̧t ɵl ꞇε tı̧m. Lɑ it on ꞇε ʃelf. Gω tɯ mı̧ ʃop and riŋ ꞇε bel. Ɛɪ ʃɑdi pωrç and kɯliŋ ʃʊur. Mɑ hqrmωni loŋ abı̧d in ʊr çurç. Fɯliʃ bơ! Ꞁhʊ dɑr hε laviʃ mı̧ muni on sω viʃus a polisi¡ Θl hɯ nω ꞇε rı̧t ʃud dɯ it.

Review.—(21.) What are the letters that may be written either upward or downward? (22.) Explain the up-stroke *r* as compared with *g*. (24.) Where are the first and third-place vowels put to the up-stroke *r*? (25.) Give the 1st rule for writing *r;* the 2d, ditto; 3d; 4th; 5th; 6th; 7th. (26.) How is it determined when the strokes *ʃ*, *r*, *l* are written upward? (27.) Give the 1st rule for writing *l;* the 2nd; 3rd; 4th; 5th? (28.) Under what circumstance is *ʃ* always written upward? What is the object of these rules? (29.) What is a word-sign? (30.) Give and describe the first-place long vowel word-signs; the third-place; the first-place short; the third-place; the diphthongs. (31.) What is the license taken with *the*?

LESSON IV.

THE CIRCLE *S* AND *Z*—*COM*, *CON*, *ING*, AND *MP*—CONSONANT WORD-SIGNS

The fact that *s* and *z* represent sounds of very frequent recurrence, renders it necessary, in order to secure the greatest brevity and beauty in writing, that they be furnished with an additional sign. Indeed, each subsequent chapter of these lessons is but to introduce some more abbreviated method of writing; which, while it seems to render the system more complex, adds to it new beauty as well as value.

32. The second forms for *s* and *z* are, a small circle, made light for the first, and thickened on one side for the latter; thus, o *s*, o *z*; the thickening of the *z* circle, however, is scarcely ever necessary, as the sense will nearly always indicate whether the circle should be *s* or *z*. Where great precision is requisite, the stroke *z* should be used.

33. The circle is used much more frequently than the stroke *s*; it is employed, however, only in connection with stroke consonants, except as a word-sign. The table on the following page will assist the learner in fixing in his mind the peculiar connection the circle has with each long sign; it will also be of great service for reference, in writing out the exercises in the lesson, if he finds any difficulty in remembering on which side of any stroke the circle should be written.

THE CIRCLE *S* AND *Z*.

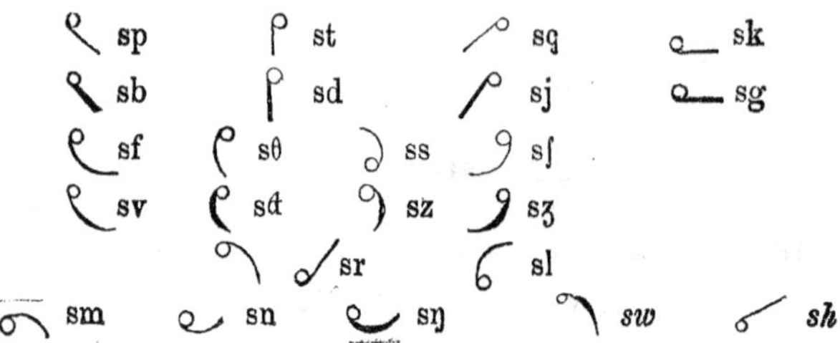

34. The stroke *y* never takes an initial circle, because not needed; it is used on its termination, however. The table presents the circle written only at the initial end of the strokes, whereas it may be written at either end, according as it is desired to read before or after the stroke; thus, *ps,* *ks,* *ws,* *hs*; and it may also, of course, be written between two strokes; thus, *kst,* *fsn.*

35. The learner must observe the following rules in writing the circle:

First. On all the straight vertical and inclined strokes, it is written on the right-hand side, both beginning and end.

Second. On the straight horizontal signs, which include the up-stroke *r*, since it is nearer horizontal than vertical, it is written on the upper side.

Third. It is written on the inner or concave side of all the curved signs. Compare the foregoing with the table.

Fourth. When it comes between two consonants it is turned in the shortest way; thus, *tsk,* *çsn,* *msn.*

36. In vocalizing words in which the circle *s* is used, the vowel-signs are to be placed to the strokes before

which or after which they read, without any reference to the circle. As rules to assist the learner, the following observations are sufficiently explicit:

First. If there be an initial circle, it is *always* read first, and then the vowel that precedes the stroke, and lastly the stroke itself, as *sɛt*, *sɵt*.

Second. If there be no vowel preceding the stroke, the circle, stroke, and following vowel are read in the order named; as *spi*, *stɷ*, *skɑl*.

Third. When the circle terminates a word, it is always the last to be read; as, *đis*, *gɷz*, *luks*, *sɛmz*, *enjɵz*, *supɷz*; when written between two strokes, the proper place for vowels can always be found; as will be seen in examining *lesun*, *eksit*.

READING EXERCISE VIII.

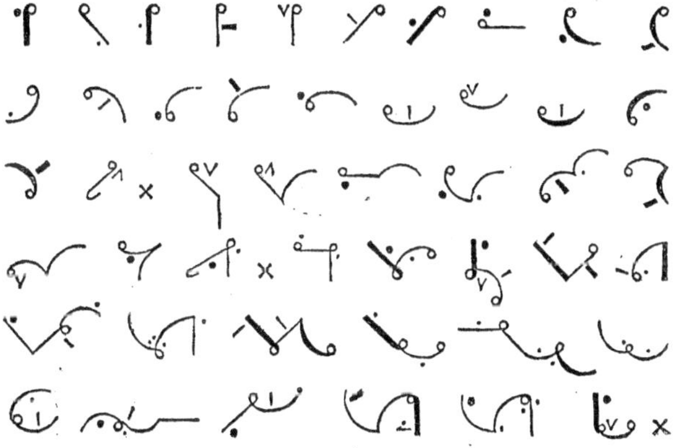

WRITING EXERCISE VIII.

Sip, sɯp, sap, sop, sɛt, sįd, sɵt, sot, sɛj, suç, sɛk, sωk, sɑv, sįđ, sɤθ, sɛz, saʃ, sur, sɤr, sel, sωl, sɑm, sum, sįn, sɯn, siŋ, suŋk. Spį, stɑ, skį, slɑ, slω, slį, snω. Pɛs, dɑz, çɛz, jɵz, gas, fɛz, vįsez. Đis, đωz, ʃɯz, rɑz, rįs, ɤrz, lɑs, mis, nįs.

Spɛk, spωk, skɛm, sfɛr, slɛp, slak, smωk, smel, snɑl, siŋk Bɛstω, bɛset, task, itself, spɑs, spesifį, skįz, siksθ, aŋkʃus, sɛdi-ʃus, risk, rɛsįt, rɛzɯn, dɛnįz, sωlles, hωlines, çωzen, mɑsɯn, fiziolωji.

---

37. There are four cases where the long *s* or *z* must always be employed: First, when it is the only stroke consonant in a word; as, *as*, *ɛz*, *sω*. Second, when it is the first consonant and preceded by a vowel; as *ask*, *ɛskap*. Third, when two distinct vowel sounds come between the *s* and following consonant; as in the word *sįens*. Fourth, when *s* or *z* is the last consonant in a word and followed by a vowel; as *ɵlsω*, *pɵlzi*. Fifth, when *z* commences a word; as *zɛl*, *Zįun*.

38 When the sound of *s* or *z* is heard twice in the same syllable, either of two forms may be used, *ss*, or *ss*; if the last sound is that of *z* the circle should be made first and the stroke be written heavy; thus, *sįz*.

39. When the indistinct vowel *i* or *e* comes between *ss* or an *s* and a *z*, or between *zz*, in the middle or at the end of a word, the syllable is represented by a circle double the usual size; thus, *pesez*, *çɯzez*, *sufįsez*, *nesesari*. It should never begin a word, as in *sistem*. In the word *eksursįz*, it is allowable to put the vowel *į* in the double circle, thus,

40. The circle is used as a word-sign for *iz*, written above the line, thus, ᴼ; and for *az*, written on the line, thus, o; with the dot aspirate prefixed they become ·ᴼ *hiz*, ·o *haz*.

READING EXERCISE IX.

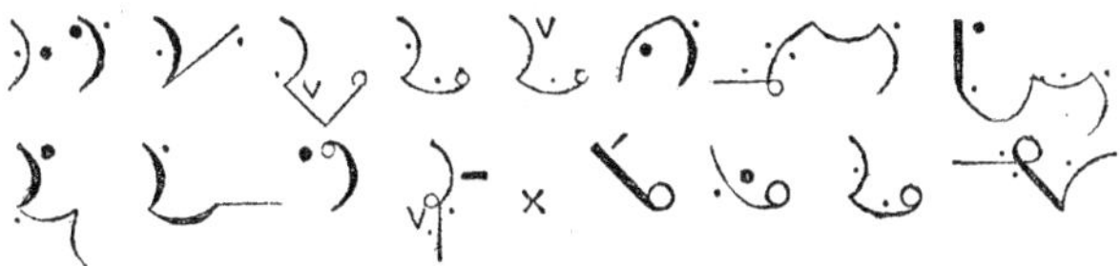

WRITING EXERCISE IX.

(37.) Ɑsa, įsi, aslɛp, espɤzal, asįnz, sįunz; bizi, spįsi, lɑzi, hɛrsɑ, ekselensi, obstinasi epilepsi, sufiʃensi; Zɷolɷji, zɛrɷ, zelusli, zigzag.

(38.) Sɛs, sez, sɛz, sizurz, sizm.

(39.) Bɑsis, dɷsez, çɯzez, kisez, diskusez, vįsez, ɤnsez, prɷpɷzez, rɛlɛsez, egzist, pozesur.

THE PREFIXES *COM* AND *CON*—THE AFFIX *ING*—*MP*.

41. For the sake of rendering Phonography as brief as possible, a few arbitrary signs are used, for the representation of prefixes and syllables in such words as would be inconvenient to write out in full. Thus, a light dot placed at the beginning of a word expresses the prefix *com* or *con*; thus, *kondem*, *konsol*; and at the end, the termination *iŋ*, when a separate syllable; as, *adiŋ*, *liviŋ*.

42. It is more convenient, however, after the *s*-circle preceded by *p*, *b*, *f*, *v*, *k*, *g*, *n*, or up-stroke *r*, to write the alphabetic *ŋ*; as *pasiŋ*, *konfesiŋ*, *rįziŋ*;

5

and after *b, bl, br, t, m;* as *nutiŋ*, *semiŋ*. Generally is written for *iŋz*; as *beiŋz*, *rejosiŋz*. A large dot may be used when more convenient; as *duiŋz*, *hediŋz*.

43. The stroke for *m* is the only one that is not given in the alphabet heavy as well as light; and in order to make good use of all the means the alphabet affords, this stroke written heavy is made to represent the not unfrequent combination of *m* with *p*, either at the beginning, middle, or end of a word; thus, *empir*, *temporari*, *lamp*.

WRITING EXERCISE X.

(41-2.) Kompar, kompil, kompoziŋ, kombat, kontaminat, konten∫us, konvinsiŋ, konva, konspir, konspirasi, konsolatori, konsul∫ip, konsurvatizm, konsiniŋ, kon∫usnes.

(43.) Pump, tempel, temporal, damp, jumpiŋ, rump, θump, simplifi, simplisiti, egzampel, romp, limp.

---

44. CONSONANT WORD-SIGNS.

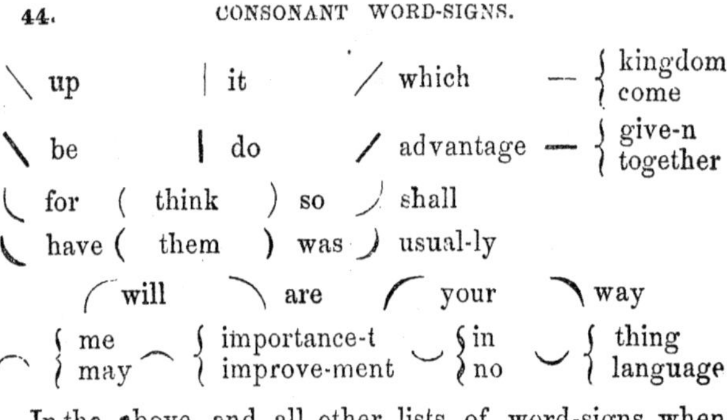

In the above, and all other lists of word-signs, when a word is printed with a hyphen, as *give-n*, the sign will represent either the whole word, or only so much as precedes the hyphen, which is, by itself, another word ; thus — is either *give* or *given.* Such words being nearly alike in sound, and yet different parts of speech, or otherwise incapable of being taken one for the other, cause no difficulty to the reader. Inasmuch as the horizontal strokes do not fill the space which a line of writing occupies, they are made to represent two words, as in the case of the vowel word-signs, one above the line and the other on the line ; these words and their respective positions are indicated in the table, by being placed one above the other, in braces, afte1 the signs.

READING EXERCISE X.

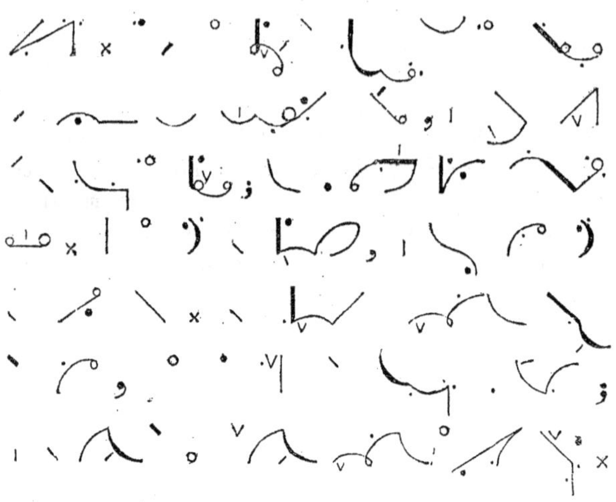

WRITING EXERCISE XI.

Ŧ lįk nɷ kiŋdum az į dɯ ɑ rɛpublik. ⁋Dɯ đɑ θiŋk đɑ wil kum up on đɛ Sinsinati mal-bɷt? Ꭿ fɛliŋ ov ɵ ʃɯd fil đį sɷl in đis hɷli hɤs. Asperiti lɯzez đɛ çɛf ov its dɛzįnz.—Hiz lɑzines iz eksesiv; hɛ dislįks hiz bɯks. Hiz fansi iz yɯʒɥali riç, and hiz dɛzįnz fɯl ov lįf. ⁋Haz đis juj nɷ justis? Onesti iz rįt polisi. Θl eskɑp tɯ đɛ siti iz hɷples. ⁋Σɯd đɛ nɑm bɛ pɯt on đɛ ɤtsįd and on đɛ top ov đɛ boks? ⁋Hɤ meni qr tɯ gɷ. It iz tɯ muç tɯ divįd amuŋ đem. Lisen tɯ đɛ lesun, and bɛ bizi, az ɑ bɷ ʃɯd bɛ, hɯ aspįrz tɯ bɛ at đɛ hed ov đɛ skɯl. Sinsɛr sorɷ iz ɛzili sɛn bɛsįd fɵls. Sɷʃal lįf givz muç hapines. Ask nɷ fasiliti in biznes afɑrz, unles it bɛ nesesɑri. Sunset sɛnuri ʃɷz riç kulurz and hansum ʃɑdz; and it çanjez intɯ meni vɑrid fɵrmz. Riçez qr sɵt bį sum, az đɛ çɛf hap-ines in đis lįf, bɛcɵz rɛali nesesɑri, az đɑ supɷz.

REVIEW.—(32.) What are the second forms for *s* and *z*? (33.) How is the circle employed? (34.) Where may it be written? (35.) On what side of the vertical and inclined strokes is it turned? Which side of the straight horizon tals? Which side of all the curves? How is it written between two strokes? (36.) How are two strokes having an *s*-circle vocalized? If there be an initial circle and preceding vowel, what is the order of reading? If vowels both precede and follow, what is the order? (37.) How many cases are there where the stroke *s* must be used? What is the 1st; 2nd; 3rd; and 4th? (38.) How should the *ss* in the same syllable be written? How *sz*? (39.) What syllables does the double circle represent? What is the exception? (40.) Designate the word-signs of the circle. (41.) What are the prefixes? The affixes? (42.) When is it more convenient to write the alphabetic *ŋ*? (43.) What is the signification of *m* made heavy? (44.) Give the words for the first eight consonant signs; for the next eight; for the next four; for the last four.

LESSON V.

IMPROPER DIPHTHONGS—*W*-HOOK—TRIPTHONGS.

W-SERIES.

long.	short.	long.	short.	Tripthongs.
wɛ	wi	wɵ	wo	Wį
wa	we	wɷ	wu	Wơ
wɑ	wa	wɯ	wɯ	Wɤ

45. The *improper diphthongs* are so termed because they consist of the union of consonants with vowels; namely, *w* and *y* with each of the twelve vowels; the improper tripthongs are the union of *w* with the diphthongs *į*, *ʊ*, and *ɤ*. The fact that *w* and *y* never occur in English except before vowels, and thus occur so frequently, induced the inventor of Phonography to represent the combined sounds by a single letter, and thus save time and space for the writer.

46. To obtain suitable characters for the representation of the *w*-series a small circle is divided perpendicularly, thus ⦶, the first or left-hand half of the circle representing the union of *w* with the first, or dot series of vowels; and like them it is made heavy for the long sounds; as *wɛp*, *wɑj*, *kwɑm*; and light for the short; as *wig*, *dwel*, *wag*.

47 The second half of the circle represents the union of *w* with the second, or dash series of vowels, heavy and light; as, *wɵrm*, *wɑv*, *wuf*, *woɡ*, *wurm*, *wud*.

48. The first-place sign of the second series of diphthongs, both long and short, when followed by *k*, up-stroke *r*, and *n*, is written in connection with such consonants; thus, *wɵk*, *wɵr*, *won*.

49. These signs should be written as small as they well can be and preserve distinct semi-circles; and, like the proper diphthongs, they must always be written vertically, and not change with the different inclinations of the consonants.

READING EXERCISE XI.

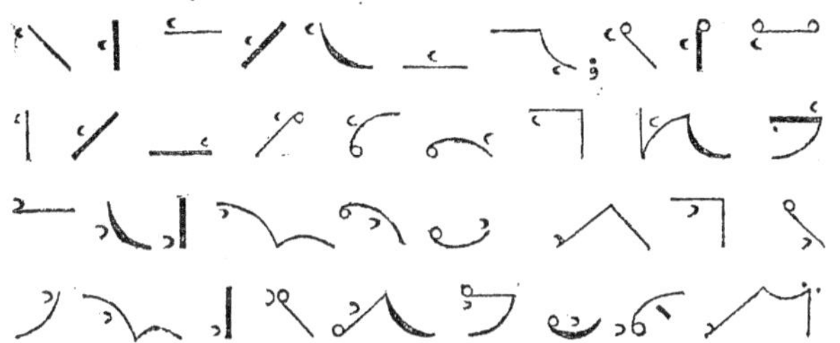

WRITING EXERCISE XII.

Wɛk, wɑt, wɑv, wɛknes, bɛwɑl, swɑr, aswɑj, wɑjez; widθ, wet, waft, wiked, swel, kwak, ekwiti, akwies, rɛliŋkwiʃ. Wɵkur, wɵk, wud, wormli, kwɵta, kwɵrum; woɡ, wud, woʃ-iŋ, skwolid, swomp. Wɵrlịk, wɵrfɑr, wɵrti, wɵkiŋstik.

50. The *W*-Hook.—The half circle, light, is joined to the first end of *l*, up-stroke *r*, *m* and *n*, to represent the simple sound of *w*; the stroke to which it is written is then vocalized as in the case of the *s*-circle; thus, *wal*, *wuri*, *wumanli*, *wan*.

51. The alphabetic sign must always be employed when *w* is the only consonant in a word, (except in the word-sign *wε*;) and in words that commence with a vowel, followed by *w*; and also when *w* is followed by *s*; thus, *wɷ*, *awak*, *Wesli*.

READING EXERCISE XII.

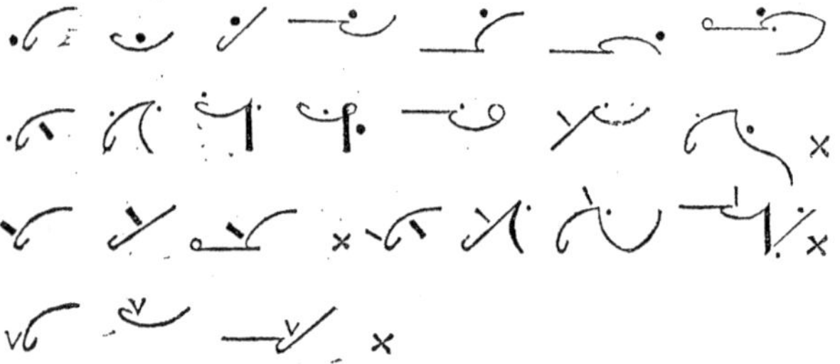

WRITING EXERCISE XIII.

Wɑliŋ, wel, wiliŋli, Wilsun, kwel, ɛkwali; Woles, wɯli; wɛri, bɛwɑr, wɑrhʊs, wɛrisum; kworel, wurk, wurkmanʃip, wurʃip, wurθles, wurȡili. Wɛmz, wompum, wɯmanlįk, skwɛmiʃnes; windɷ, kwenç, twenti, twinj, entwįn. Wįr, kwɛri, inkwįr, wel-beiŋ, skwolur, elɷkwens, ɛkwanimiti. Wɯ, awɑr, wįzli.

---

52. Tripthongs.—The characters with which to represent the combination of *w* with the diphthongs, are obtained by dividing a small square thus, ; the first right-angle

representing the tripthong *wį*, the second, *wɤ*, and the second put to the first place, *wɵ*; thus, *wįf*, *kwɵt*. Since the introduction of the *w*-hook to *r*, *l*, *m*, *n*, the *wɤ* character is not needed. Sometimes may be connected with the following consonant; as *wįd*, *wįf*.

53. By placing the aspirate before these improper diphthongs and tripthongs, we get the proper representation of the first two sounds in such words as *wheat*, *whig*, *while*, (the *w* coming before the *h* in the old orthography being an inversion of the order of the elements in speaking the words;) thus, *hwεt*, *hwig*.

54. When the *w*-hook is used, the aspirate is indicated by making the hook heavy; thus, *hwεl*, *hwɑr-fɷr*. But when the alphabetic *w* is employed, the aspirate is indicated by a small tick, thus, *hwiz*.

READING EXERCISE XIII.

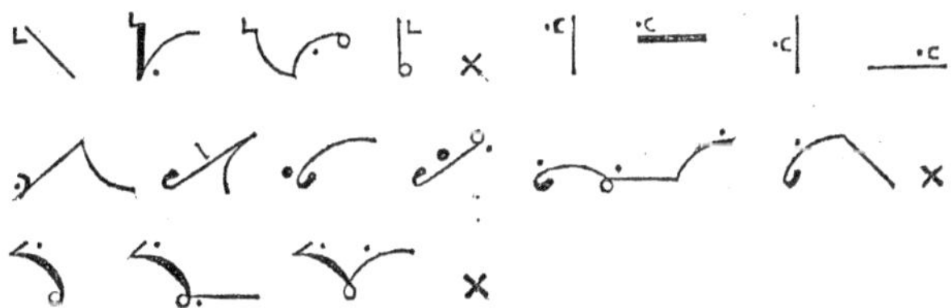

WRITING EXERCISE XIV.

Wįvz, kwįet, wįdnes, kwįetnes, kwɷt, Irikwɷ.

Hwip, hwįt, hwiguri; hwɑrbį, hwɑrwid, hwɑrat, hwurlpɯl, enihwɑr, nɷhwɑr; hwεlbarɷ, hwεlrįt, hwalur, hwimzikaliti, hwεlm; hwens, hwįn; hwiskur hwislur.

5. *W* WORD-SIGNS.

we	with	what	why	when
were	would	where	while	one
				well

These word-signs, like the simple vowel-signs, are to be written above or on the line, as their positions in the table indicate.

READING EXERCISE XIV.

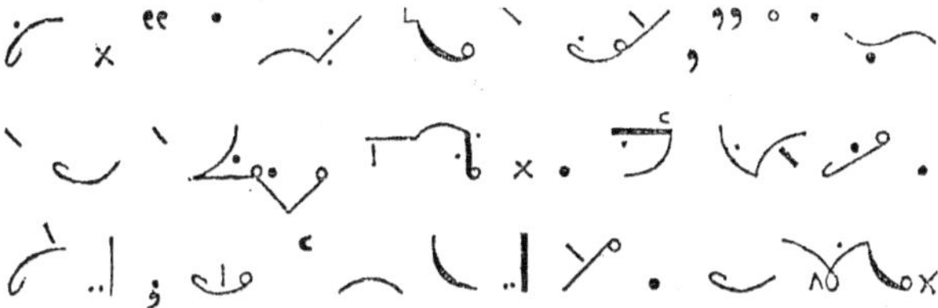

WRITING EXERCISE XV.

Bɛwar ov ᵭɛ wɉn kup. Ꭿ wɉz ꞔɵs. Wɛ wɯd bɛ hapi wiᵭ hiz kumpani. ꝗHwɉ ʃɯd wɛ kil and ɛt swɉn. ꝗHwot iz hiz wiʃ, and hwar wɯd hɛ gɷ. Hwɉ, ɋ! hwɉ, mɉ sɷl, ᵭis aŋgwiʃ. Ɨ gɷ awa hwar wɷ and aŋkʃus kar dɯ not asal eni wun. Wɯd ɉ wur at hɷm. Wɵr wurks mizuri, hwɉl pɛs givz kɋm rɛpɷz tɯ ɵl.

THE Y-SERIES.

long.	short.	long.	short.
yɛ	yi	ye	yo
ya	ye	yɷ	yu
yɑ	ya	yɯ	yu

56. To obtain characters to represent the *y*-series of improper diphthongs, the small circle is taken and divided horizontally, thus, -⊖-; the under half represents the dot group of vowels, and is made heavy for the long sounds; as, *yɛr*, *Yal*, *Yɑzɯ*; and light for the short; as, *yis*, (a common but not approved pronunciation of *yes*,) *yel*, *yam*; the upper half represents the union of *y* with the dash group of vowels, heavy and light; as, *yol*, *yɷk*, *yɯs*; *yon*, *yuŋ*; *y* never occurs before *u* in the English language.

57. In writing, the same rules must be observed in regard to these signs as with the *w*-series. (48)

58. Word Signs.— ye, yet, beyond, yɯ.

READING EXERCISE XV.

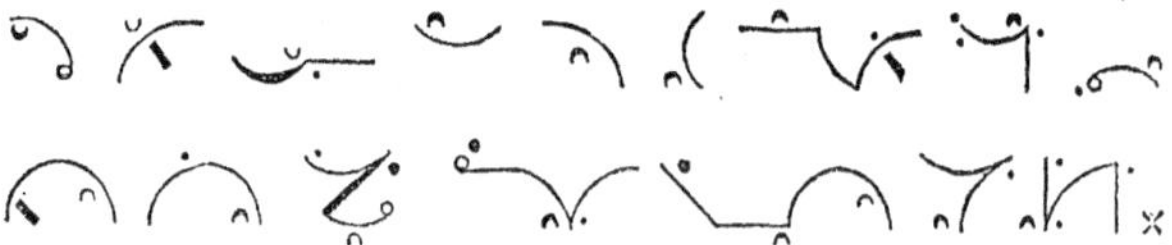

WRITING EXERCISE XVI.

NOTE.—In Phonography, 'ɥ' in the following lessons may be written as 'yɯ.'

Yɛrli, yɛn, yɛrliŋ, yelɷiʃ, yelpiŋ, yɷmanri, Yokigani, yuŋiʃ, Nɥ Yɵrk, hɥj, sɥt, amɥz, rɛdɥs, dɥti, rɛfɥz, kontɥmli, anyɯal. Ƌɛ yɯtƀ ov ɤr komyɯniti ʃɯd ɛɑ̧ ɕɯz sum fɑr egzampel, and folɷ it kontinyɯali. Pɥr simplisiti givz mɛ jơ. Ƌis Manyɯal ʃɯd bɛ yɯr gȷd. It iz ɑ wurk ov yɯtiliti.

READING EXERCISE XVI.

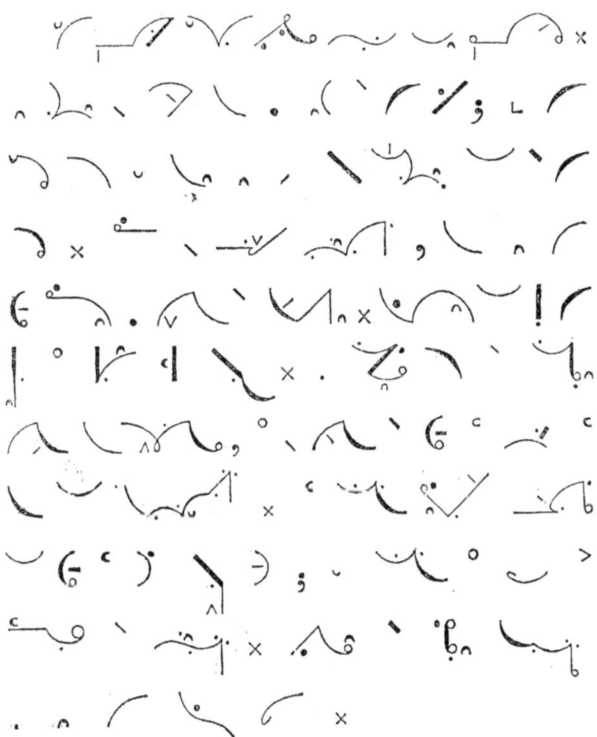

WRITING EXERCISE XVII.

Nɥ Yɵrk iz ɑ popyɯlus siti. Yɯ nɷ hɯ ɩ am, yet ɩ am at ɑ los tɯ spɛk yɯr nɑm. Hɥmaniti ʃɯd liv in pɛs az wun komyɯniti; đɑ ʃɯd dwel tɯgeđur in ɵl đɛ urt in hqrmɷni and luv. If yɯ mɑk fɑlyurz in dɥti, yɯ wil rɛsɛv đɛ laʃ ov justis. Đɛ nɥz-bɷ amɥzez himself hwɩl wɵkiŋ. Hɷ yes! hɷ yes! sez đɛ yuŋ bel riŋur. Đɛ yɷk ov đɛ oks iz hevi; it gɵlz hiz nek đis wɵrm dɑ. In dɑz ov yɷr, hwen wɛ wer yuŋ.

Wɛ yɯʒɥali giv đem ɑt ɤrz fɵr slɛpiŋ, ten fɵr wurk, and siks hwiç đɑ mɑ imprɯv in eni wɑ. Đɛ bɷz ɩ am tɛçiŋ qr dɛzɩrus ov imprɯvment; đɑ sɛm tɯ tiŋk in đis wɑ—hwot iz wurt dɯiŋ at ɵl, iz wurt dɯiŋ wel. Ɩ hɷp đɑ wil ɵlwɑz liv up tɯ đis maksim, sɷ ʃal đɑ hav sukses in lɩf. Sun, giv mɛ yɯr ɛr, and ɩ wil tɛç yɯ đɛ wɑ ov lɩf. Leŋt ov dɑz iz given us fɵr sɷʃal and rɛlijus imprɯvment.

Review.—(45.) Explain the improper diphthongs; the tripthongs. (46.) How are the former represented? Which series of vowels, combined with *w*, does the left-hand half of the circle represent? (47.) What are the sounds of the right-hand half of the circle? (48.) To what consonants may the signs for *we* and *wo* be written without lifting the pen? (50.) To what strokes does the *w* semi-circle connect and form a hook? On which side of the up-stroke *r* is it written? How does it differ in power from the improper diphthongs? (51.) When must the alphabetic *w* be employed? (52.) Designate the representation of the tripthongs. (53.) What is the phonographic representation of *wh?* (54.) How is the *w*-hook aspirated? (55.) Designate the first line of word-signs; the second.

(56.) What are the signs to represent the *y*-series? Which half of the circle represents the dot series? What are their sounds? What are the sounds of the upper half? (57.) How are they to be written to the consonants? (58.) What are the word-signs?

LESSON VI.

INITIAL HOOKS — THE *L* HOOK EXPLAINED.

59. A peculiar characteristic of *l* and *r* is, that they readily unite with preceding consonants,—they flow back into them, as it were; and hence their classification as liquids. This union, though a kind of double sound, is formed by a single effort of the voice. Take, for illustration, the two words *play* and *pray*, and observe how simultaneously the *pl* and *pr* are spoken; so in the termination of the words *title* and *acre*; in the former class of words no vowel sound comes between the two consonants, of course; in the latter a very indistinct one is heard, but which it is not necessary to represent in Phonography.

60. For the purpose of farther abbreviating phonographic writing, this combining of *l* and *r* with previous consonants is represented by hooks written to those consonants. As the long consonants are heard first in the words, consistency would seem to require that they be written first and the hooks afterward; but the reverse of this is the case, for the reason that hooks on the termination of the strokes maybe more philosophically and advantageously employed for other purposes; and besides, the *pl*, *pr*, *bl*, *br*, &c., being considered single sounds almost, the stroke and the hook may be regarded in the same light; they should actually be spoken as such in spelling and reading, i. e., as the final syllables in *able*, (*bl*) *little*, (*tl*) *paper*, (*pr*) *lover*, (*vr*); and not as *p*, *l*; *b*, *l*; *p*, *r*; *b*, *r*.

TABLE OF THE *L*-HOOK.

pl	tl	ʃl	kl
bl	dl	jl	gl
fl	ŧl	ʃl } struck up.	
vl	đl	ʒl }	

61. The hook is first turned, and then the long consonant struck in the usual manner. The *l*-hook, like the *s*-circle, is made on the right-hand side of the vertical and inclined straight strokes, on the upper side of the straight horizontals, and on the inside of the curves.

62. This hook to the strokes *s*, *z*, down-stroke *r* and *ŋ* is not needed, since for *sl* and *zl*, the circle is used with more advantage; as, *sla*, *muzel;* and the initial hook to *l*, up-stroke *r*, *m* and *n*, is more useful as *w*.

63. The *ʃ* and *ʒ* take the *l*-hook only when they are combined with other stroke consonants, and then they are *struck upward;* thus, *esenʃal*, *ambroʒal*.

64. The stroke and the hook being considered as *one sign*, are vocalized as though no hook were used; and in writing, if a vowel precedes a hooked stroke it is written before it; thus, *abel*, *evil;* and if the vowel follows, it must be placed after; thus, *pla*, *klos;* or a vowel may be written both before and after; thus, *abli*, *idlur*, *deklar*, *eksklam*.

65. In some combinations of consonants it is difficult to make a good *l*-hook, but it can generally be understood, as in the word *repli;* in some cases, however, it is necessary to write the long *l;* as in *suksesful*.

Note.—The learner must remember that the hook *l* is to be used only when its sound follows a preceding stroke consonant; hence *lp*, *ld*, *lk*, *&c.*, must be written with the stroke *l*.

READING EXERCISE XVII.

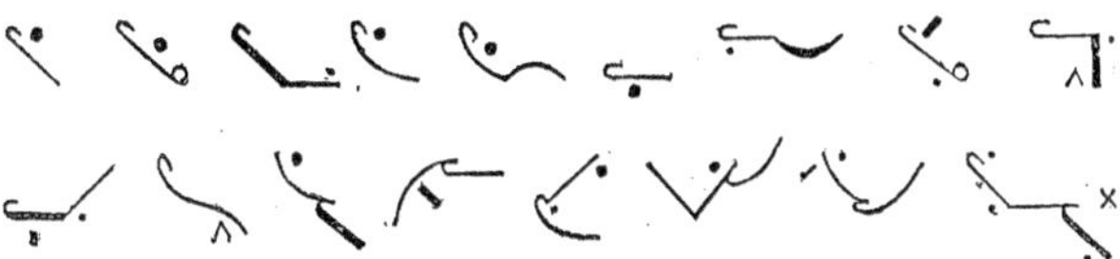

WRITING EXERCISE XVIII.

Pla, blω, glɛ, flį, plɤ, aplį, ωblįj, aflikt, bįbel, tįtel, kupel, plenti, blȧzez, klȧsez, rɛgal, fïkel, rɛklam, inflȧm, rɛmɯval, fȧtal, radikal, klerikal, buʃel, espeʃal, mqrʃal, influɯenʃal.

SPECIAL SCHEME OF VOCALIZATION.

66. It has been stated, (59) that the *l*-hook is designed to be used when no vowel comes between the sound of *l* and a preceding consonant, or when the vowel is but indistinctly heard; of the latter class are the following: *apelz*, *egelz*; of this class of words, however, it is held by some that there is no vowel sound heard in the last syllables. But it is found very convenient, occasionally, to take a little license with the rule, and use the hook even where a vowel sound is distinctly heard between it and the stroke. Thus, in writing the word *falsehood*, it is much easier and quicker to write the hook *l*; thus, than thus, .

67. When this is done, a peculiar scheme of vocalization is resorted to; namely, the dot vowels are indicated by a small circle placed in the three positions, before the stroke for the long, and after for the short vowels; as *delɥsiv*, *til*, *legal*; when the dash vowels are to be read between the stroke and the hook, it is indicated by striking the dash through the stroke; as *kulpabel;* or

when its place is at the hooked end it may be written just before the hooked stroke; thus, *tolurabel;* the diphthongs, when necessary, are written as the stroke vowels; thus, *gıldiʃ,** *kwolifı.*

This method of writing is used to a very limited extent; and the learner is cautioned against using it for any words but such as are designated, in this and subsequent lessons, to be written thus.

READING EXERCISE XVIII.

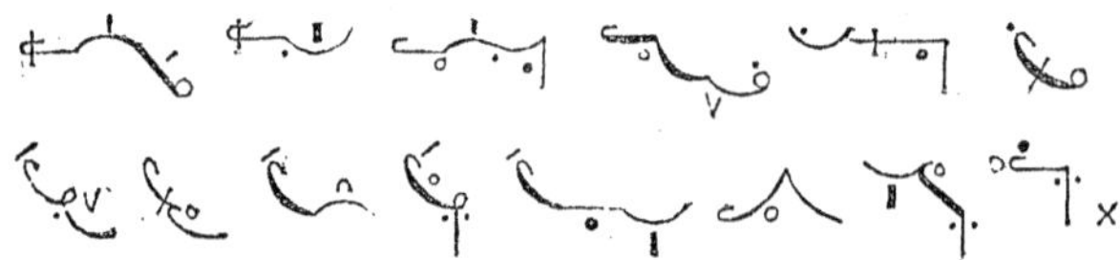

WRITING EXERCISE XIX.

Felsiti, fulzkap, felɷ-sitizenz, fulnes, fulminat, vulgat, filɷsofikal, voluptųus, konvulsiv, kolɷnial, galvanik, kalamiti, kolekt, kalkųlat, ʃiliŋ.

L-HOOK PRECEDED BY THE *S*-CIRCLE.

68. The *s*-circle is prefixed to the compound consonant signs, as well as to the simple. It is first written, and the pen carried round so as to form the hook before making the long sign; thus, *supel,* *sagel,* *siviliz.*

69. No new rules are required for vocalizing; it needs only to be borne in mind when the long *s* is to be used (37); and that the stroke and hook are considered as one sign, and if the vowel is heard before them it is written before them; if after, it is written afterward; as in the previous examples.

---

*See Lesson X, on Half-length Strokes.

70. In reading, the circle is read first, then the vowel, if one precede the compound stroke; and lastly the compound consonant, with its following vowel if there be one.

71. Word-signs. *kol*, *difikulti*, *ful*, *til* and *tel*, *valyu*.

READING EXERCISE XIX.

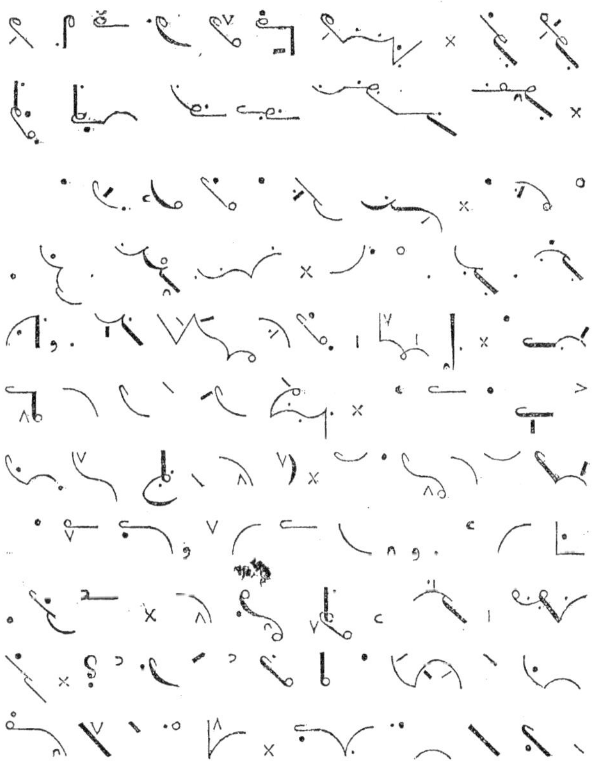

WRITING EXERCISE XX.

Setel, sįdel, sutelti, sikelz, siviliti, supelnes, siviljziŋ, swivel, spljsiŋ, pɛsful, posibel, splendid, fɛzabel, advjzabel, displaiŋ, disklωzez.

ƗDELNES.—Ɨdelnes iz a plag tu đɛ skolur, fɵr unles hɛ aplįz himself klωsli tu hiz buks, hɛ luzez ɵl klam tu đɛ aplɵz ov hiz famili ɵr hiz ofiʃal sųpɛriur. It iz ʃamful; fɵr hɛ ʃud rekolekt đat hiz famili hav a rįt tu luk fɵr sumtiŋ yusful in him tu rɛpa đem fɵr tɵl and aŋzįeti. It iz unrɛzunabel; fɵr, unles hɛ giv up hiz ɛvil wa and du hiz dųti fatfuli, nω blesiŋ awats him, but hɛ iz displɛziŋ tu hiz klasfelωz, tu himself, and tu ɵl pɛpel. Fįnali, it iz ɵful; fɵr įdel habits qr apt tu bɛkum wurs, and đɛ ɛvil wun "ɵlwaz misçif sɛks fɵr įdel yut tu du." But đɛ skolur hu fatfuli aplįz himself tu wurk, wil ωblįj him hu tɛçez him, and plɛz ɵl pɛpel hu nω him.

REVIEW.—(59.) Explain the peculiar character of *l* and *r*. (60.) How are strokes with *l* and *r*-hooks to be spoken? (61.) On which side of the vertical and inclined straight strokes is the *l*-hook written? Which side of the straight horizontals? Which side of the curves? (62.) To which of the strokes is the *l*-hook not written, and why? (63.) How do ʃ and ʒ take the *l*-hook? (64.) How are *l*-hook strokes vocalized? (66.) What is said about a vowel sound between the stroke consonant and the hook? (67.) How are vowels of the dot series represented in the scheme for vocalizing the hook? How the dash series? How the dipthongs? (68.) How may the *s*-circle be written to the initial end of the hooked strokes? (70.) What is the rule for reading such compound strokes? (71.) What are the *l*-hook word-signs?

LESSON VII.

THE *R*-HOOK — DOUBLE CURVE FOR *ar*.

72. The *r*-hook is written on the left-hand side of the vertical and inclined straight strokes, and on the under side of the straight horizontals,—just the reverse of the *l*-hook. Some of the curved strokes take this hook irregularly.

TABLE OF THE *R*-HOOK.

pr	tr	çr	kr
br	dr	jr	gr
fr	ŧr	ʃr	
vr	đr	ʒr	
mr		nr	

73. It will be seen from the table that *f, v, ŧ* and *đ* take the *r*-hook by assuming the positions of *r, w, s* and *z;* thus, *fre,* *ovur,* *ŧru,* *eđur,* which they can do without danger of ambiguity, since these letters never receive an initial hook: *rr* not being wanted, *wr* existing in the *w*-hook to the up-stroke *r*, and the *sr zr* being supplied by the *s*-circle; thus, , and

74. To indicate the *r*-hook on *m* and *n*, the strokes are made heavy, which distinguishes them from *wm wn;* thus, *onur,* *dinur,* *gramur; ŋ* does not take any hook, and hence *n* made heavy with a hook will not make confusion.

Sometimes this hook, like the *l*-hook, has to be made rather indistinctly, as *degre.* *askrib.* After the downward *r* is used instead of the hook, as *fakur.*

75. The remarks in regard to vocalizing the *l*-hook strokes apply in every particular to the *r*-hook strokes. It should especially be borne in mind that the hooked strokes are regarded as one letter, and spoken as the last syllables in rea*per*, let*ter*, a*cre*, &c.; and that as a general thing the hook is only used when no distinct vowel sound comes between another consonant and a following *r*; as in *pra*, *kru*, *utur*, *lezur*.

76. When is preceded by (*wo*), they may be united; as in *wotur*, and all its compounds.

READING EXERCISE XX.

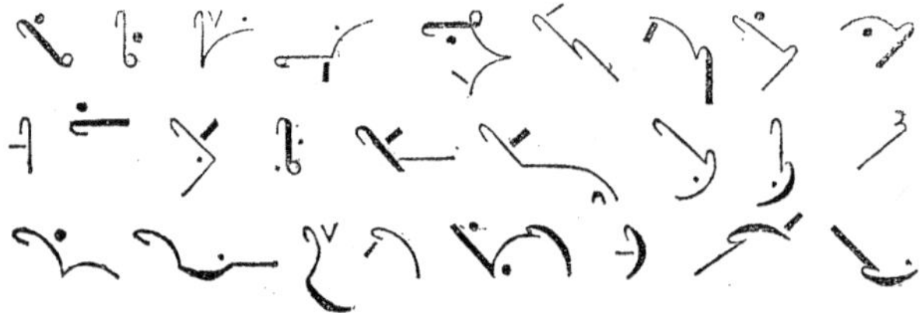

WRITING EXERCISE XXI.

Drį, trɛ, drɑ, krį, grω, ɑkur, ωdur, upur, aprįz, ɑpril, ɑprɯv, drɛm, brij, frɛk, frįdɑ, mɯvur, klωvur, ŧrω, gađur, plezur, ɛrɑzur, plumur, murdur, manur, onurabel, ωvurluk evuri-hwɑr, kriminal, purçesez, transpωz, trembel, brudur, jurni, jurnal, frɑmur, Fransis, wundurfɯl. Ȼekur, jωkur.

77. A limited license is taken with the above rule(75), as in the case of the *l*-hook, and the *r*-hook is used when a distinct vowel sound does come between it and the previous consonant; in which case the same peculiar scheme of vocalization is employed; thus, *Der sur*, *dqrk*, *pursun*, *kωrs*, *rɛkwįrz*, *postyur*.

READING EXERCISE XXI.

WRITING EXERCISE XXII.

Ɛɛrfɯl, kɐrles, mɛrli, nɛrli, Ɛɋrlz, ɕɋrkɷl, paragraf, ʃɋrk, ʃɋrpur, ŧərni, purvurs, kɷrsli, moraŀiti, nərŧ, nuriʃ, ɛnorṃiti, prɛliminɐri, fɛtyur, lɛktyur.

THE *R*-HOOK PRECEDED BY THE *S*-CIRCLE.

78. The *s*-circle precedes the *r*-hook in much the same manner as it does the *l*-hook; thus, it might be written *spr*, *skr;* but since the *s*-circle alone never occupies the *r*-hook side of the straight strokes, advantage is taken of the circumstance, since a circle is more easily written than a circle and a hook, to write simply the circle; thus, *stra*, *skrɛm*, *sịdur*, *sukur*, *sɛjur*. But with the curves this contraction cannot be made, since the simple *s*-circle occupies the place; hence the circle and hook must both be written; thus *sufur*, *sumur*, *sinur*.

79. When the *s*-circle and *r*-hook come between two straight consonants, it is often more convenient to write the hook in addition to the circle than not; as in *prospur*, *ekstra*.

80. The same rules are to be observed in vocalizing and reading that were given for the *l*-hook preceded by the *s* circle, (68, 69.)

READING EXERCISE XXII.

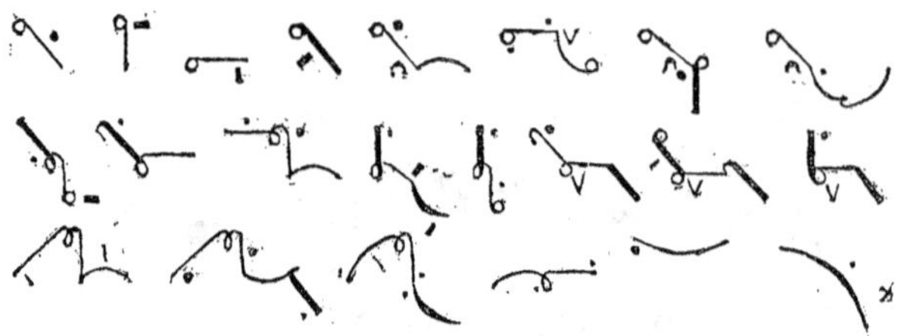

WRITING EXERCISE XXIII.

Sprȷ̧, strɑ, strȷ̧k, strɐm, skrɐp, skrɯpel, skrȷ̧b, streŋt, strugel stranj, stroŋgur, supur, sɐbur, sɥpremasi, sɐkrɛsi, sȷ̧fur, sufuriŋ, sevur, simur, sɯnur.

THE DOUBLE CURVE FOR *ƋR*.

81. When a curved stroke is repeated, an angle is made between the two; thus, *ff*, *nn*, which leaves at liberty, to be used for some other purpose, the *double-length* strokes. A somewhat arbitrary, though convenient use, is made of them thus: Doubling the length of a curved stroke, adds the syllable *ƌur* to the single strokes; thus, *fɑƌur*, *anuƌur*. These forms are used chiefly as word-signs for *fɑƌur*, *muƌur*, *neƌur*, (above the line,) *anuƌur*, *raƌur*, *furƌur*.

---

82. *R*-HOOK WORD-SIGNS.

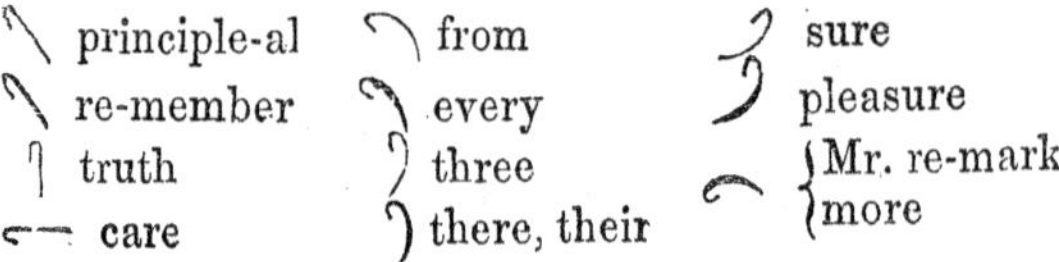

principle-al — from — sure
re-member — every — pleasure
truth — three — Mr. re-mark
care — there, their — more

READING EXERCISE XXIII.

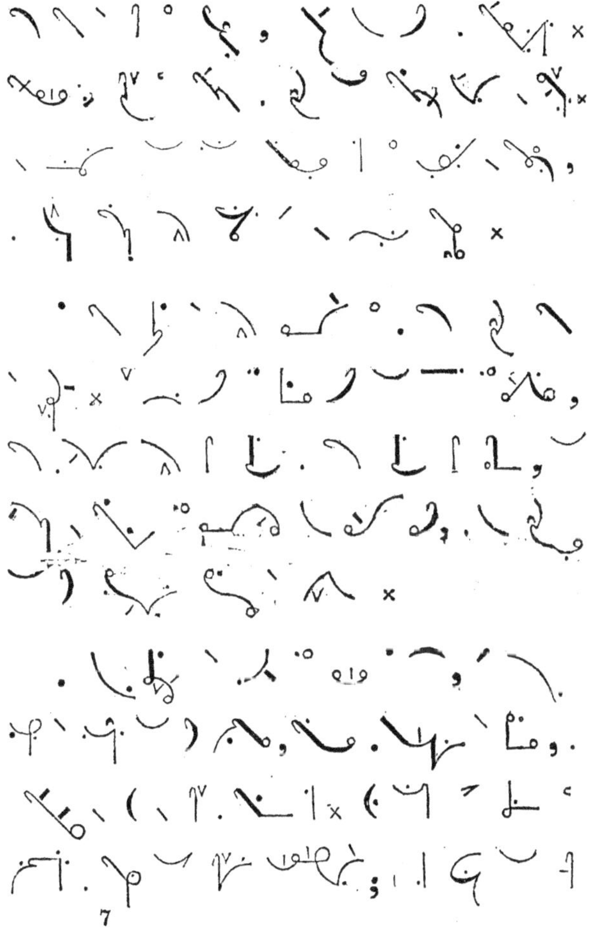

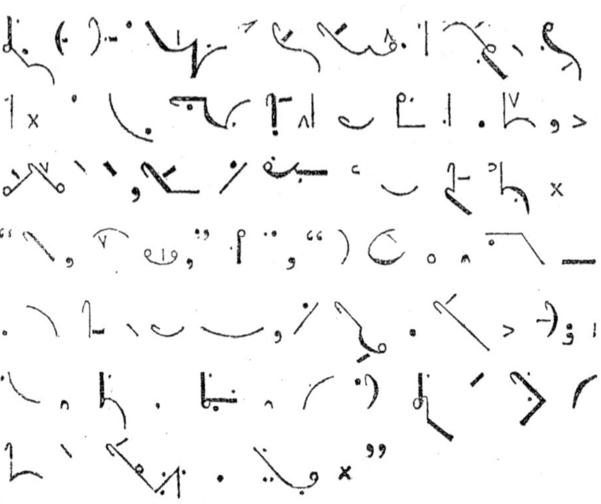

WRITING EXERCISE XXIV.

Sɛriusnes and Sωbrieti.—Nu'iŋ nωbel iz tɯ bɛ had but wiđ sɛriusnes and sωbrįeti. Ɛ sωbur pursun sɛks tɯ wɑ đɛ trɯ valyɯ ov ŧiŋz and tɯ lɑ nω trezurz in trįfelz, but rađur on hwot iz impɵrtant. Nuŧiŋ, puhaps, strįks us az sω strɑnj and fɯliʃ az tɯ obzurv pɛpel sɛrius abɤt trįfelz, and trįfliŋ wiđ sɛrius ŧiŋz. Sωsįeti sufurz konsidurabli bį đɛ trįflur, hɯ hɑts sωbrįeti and sɛriusnes, and wɯd sɯnur hav foli tɯ rɯl sųprɛm. Suplįd wiđ strɵz tɯ plɑ wiđ, hɛ sufurz đɛ strɛm ov lįf tɯ flω awɑ, until deŧ pɯts in hiz sikel, and separɑts đɛ striŋ ov lįf. Nɤ iz nω tįm fɵr sukur ɵr eskɑp. Hɛ strįks wiđ streŋŧ and uneriŋ ɑm; strips him ov ɵl hiz plɛz, strɯz hiz hωps intɯ đɛ ɑr, and ɑ strugel klωzez hiz karɛr. It iz bωŧ untrɯ and strɑnj tɯ konstrɯ sɛriusnes intɯ sadnes, ɵr tɯ konsidur sωbrįeti đɛ sam az unhapines; fɵr it iz skɑrsli posibel tɯ bɛ propurli gɑ ɵr trɯli hapi, unles wɛ nω hwen tɯ bɛ sωbur.

Review.—[72] On which side of the straight strokes is the *r*-hook written? [73.] What strokes do not take the *r*-hook? In what way do *f*, *v*, *ŧ*, *đ*, take the *r*-hook? Why this irregularity? (74.) How do *m* and *n* take this hook? (75.) What is said about vocalizing? (77.) What is the license in regard to the use of the *r*-hook? Explain the peculiar scheme of vocalization. (78.) How is the *s*-circle prefixed to the straight *r*-hook strokes? How to the curves? (80.) What is the rule for reading these combinations? (81.) What is effected by doubling the length of curved strokes? [82.] Designate the first four word-signs; the next four; the last five.

LESSON VIII.

TERMINAL HOOKS.

83. Since the hooked strokes, although representing two elementary sounds, are written with nearly the same facility as the simple strokes, the method of hooking is applied to the termination of the consonant signs as well as to the beginning. The most useful purposes which the two terminal hooks can subserve, are to represent the very frequent sound of *n* and the common final syllable *ʃun*, heard in such words as *passion, nation, physician,* &c.

TABLE OF THE *N*-HOOK.

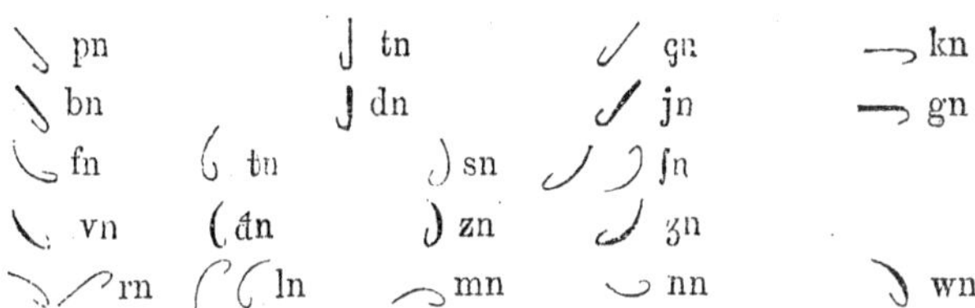

84. On the straight strokes the *n*-hook is written on the same side that the *r*-hook occupies; that is, on the left hand side of the vertical and inclined, and on the under side of the horizontal strokes, embracing, of course, the up-stroke *r*; while on the curves it is written on the inner or concave side, whether to the left or right; as illustrated in the preceding table.

85. The *n*-hook might be written on all the strokes; but on the *y* it would seldom, if ever, be of any advantage. The *w*-hook to the *w* answers every purpose that an *n*-hook to the *w* would; the *h* with a final hook would not be so serviceable as the dot aspirate.

86. Of the two forms for *ln*, *ʃn*, the down-stroke *ʃ* and the up-stroke *l* are generally used, the others being employed only in connection with other strokes when the first mentioned would be unhandily written.

87. The *n*-hook is always the last thing, belonging to a stroke, to be read; thus, *pan*, *fin*, *ŧin*, *ɖin*, *run*, *lin*. If no distinct vowel sound is heard between the stroke and the hook, no vowel sign is written; as, *heven*, *ɷʃan;* where a third-place vowel sound is heard, the sign must be placed on the outside of the hook; thus, *man*, *ɖan*, *wagun*; thus the vocalization is the same as in other compound strokes.

88. Strokes having an initial circle or hook, of any kind, may also have a final hook or circle; as *plan*, *stran*.

89. When the *n* is the last consonant in a word, followed by a vowel, it must be written at length; as *muni*, *Cina*.

READING EXERCISE XXIV.

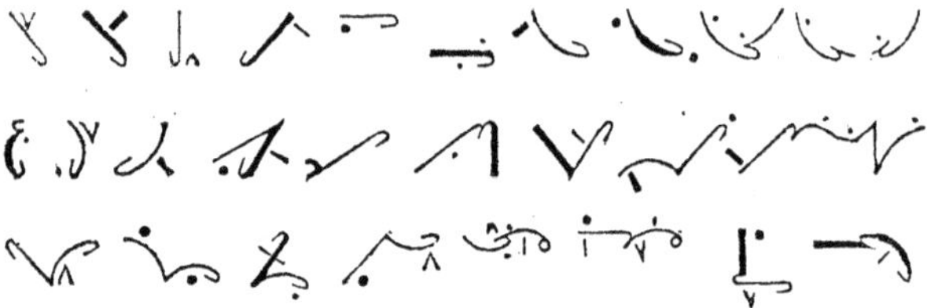

WRITING EXERCISE XXV.

Pan, pin, bɯn, tɷn, dɤn, ȼan, jɵn, kan, gon, fɉn, van ɖen, ʃɉn, ɷʃan, ran, run, lɷn, lɉn, mɉn, mɯn, nɷn, nɤn; ɷpen, rɉpen, gɋrden, ʃaken, ɵrgan, ɵrfan, enlɉven, mɷrn, wɵrniŋ, fɵlen, balɯn, rɷman, wɯman. Brɤn, dran, restran, pɋrdun, burden, rɛfran, rɛgan, enjɵn, abstan.

THE *N*-HOOK FOLLOWED BY *S*.

90. When *s* follows after *n*, without an intervening vowel, the circle may be turned on the hook, as in the case of *s* preceding the *l*-hook and *r*-hook; thus, *fanz*, *vịnz*, *manz*, *maʃenz*, *refranz*. With the straight strokes, however, it is unnecessary to make both the hook and circle, since the circle itself embraces the hook, and will not be mistaken for *s*, which is always written on the other side of the stroke; thus, *penz*, *duns*, *ganz*, *mornz*, *beginz*.

91. The double circle for *nsez* is conveniently used on the straight strokes, for such words as *tensez*, *gansez*, *konsekwensez*; but as a double circle cannot well be formed on the hook attached to a curve, a stroke *n* must be used in such words as *finansez* *evinsez*.

READING EXERCISE XXV.

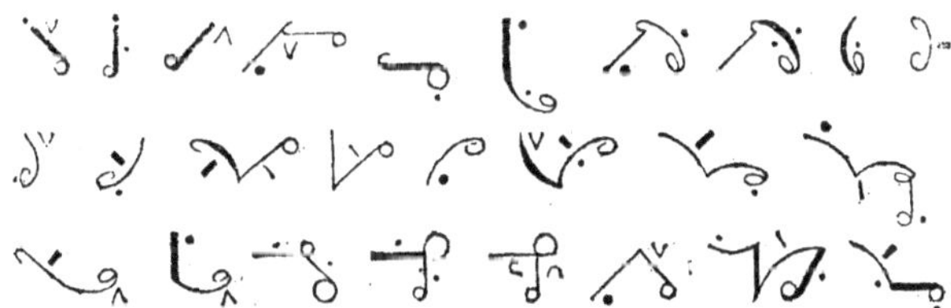

WRITING EXERCISE XXVI.

Panz, benz, penz, tonz, ganz, ganz, mornz, burnz, erfanz vịnz, ʃunz, balans, remanz, Jurmanz, pronsns; komplanz, eksplanz, akerdans, kwestyunz, kristyanz, enjenz, inklịnz. Prinsez, dansez, kondensez, glansez, ekspensez, konsekwensez, pronsnsez, advansez, konʃensez.

92. N-HOOK WORD-SIGNS.

upon	can	than
been	phonography	alone
done	phonographer	men
generally	phonographic	opinion

READING EXERCISE XXVI.

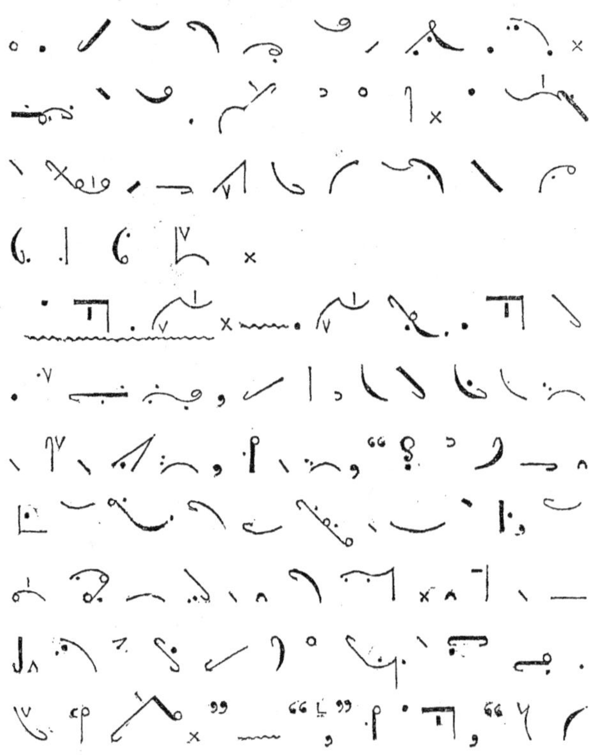

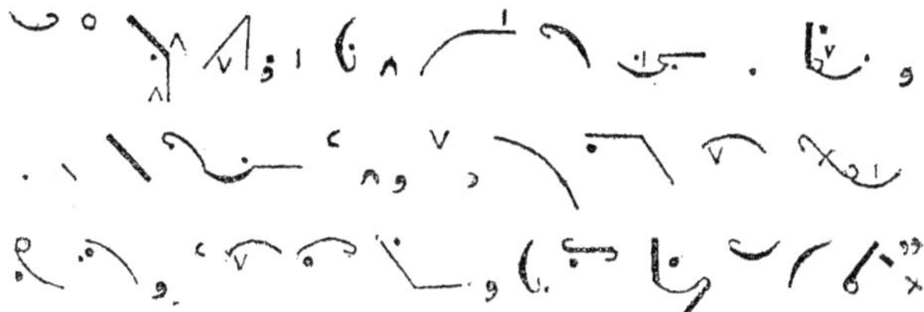

WRITING EXERCISE XXVII.

KUREJ.—Trɯ kurej haz its orijen in vurtʮ. Animal fɛrlɛsnes pɯts on ɗɛ semblans ov kurej, and iz ofen tɐken fər it, bʝ nʝn ɤt ov ten amuŋ men; but ɗɛ falasi ov ɗis ɷpinyun haz bin ʃɷn bʝ jenural ekspɛriens, fər prɯdens iz ɛkwali esenʃal tɯ it. Tɯ atɐn trɯ kurej, entur upon nuɬiŋ raʃli, egzamin wel hwot ɗɛ iʃyɯ iz lʝkli tɯ bɛ, and fərm yɯr ɷpinyun bɛfɷr yɯ bɛgin. ꟸHɤ kan yɯ ɗen fɛr, if yɯ hav gon tɯ wurk upon prinsipel, and hav dun ɵl yɯ kan dɯ; ər ꟸhwʝ ʃɯd yɯ fɛl ɐ konsurn fər konsɛkwensez, hwiç hav bin ɵlredi wɐd bʝ yɯ. In humbel rɛlʝans upon ɗɛ asistans ov Heven, gɷ ɷpenli and wiɗ konfidens tɯ finiʃ yɯr planz. Ɑis simpel faɬ alɷn, ɗɛ rɛlʝans ov çildren upon ɐ Hevenli Fɑɗur, wil kari yɯ sɐfli ɬrɯ. Rɛmembur ɗis trɯɬ, hɤevur, ɗɐr iz jenurali mɷr trɯ kurej ʃɷn bʝ ɐ pasiv rɛzistans tɯ ɗɛ skərn and snɛrz ov men, ɗan haz evur bin sɛn in eni bodili dɛfens hwotsɷevur. Trɯ kurej iz bʝ nɷ mɛnz savej vʝɷlens, nər ɐ fɯl-hɑrdi insensibiliti tɯ danjur; nər ɐ hedstroŋ raʃnes tɯ run sudenli intɯ it; nər ɐ burniŋ frenzi brɷken lɯs from ɗɛ guvurniŋ pɤur ov rɛzun; but it iz ɐ sɛrɛn, furm deturminiŋ—ɗɛ kurej ov ɐ man, but nevur ɗɛ fɛrsnes ov ɐ tʝgur.

REVIEW.—(83.) What are final hooks? (84.) On which side of the straight strokes is the *n*-hook written? On which side of the curves? (85.) On what strokes is the *n*-hook not written? (86.) Which forms of the *ln* and *ʃn* are generally used? (87.) How are the *n*-hook strokes vocalized? (89.) In what case must the stroke *n* be employed? (90.) How is the circle written to the *n*-hook on the curves? How on the straight strokes? (91.) What is the double circle when written in the *n*-hook place? (92.) Designate the straight stroke word-signs; the curved strokes.

LESSON IX.

ƩN-HOOK—VOWEL CONTRACTIONS—DISSYLLABIC DIPHTHONGS.

93. This hook is entirely arbitrary; that is, it is not phonetic at all, in that it is but one sign used to represent three sounds; but it is nevertheless more consistent than the old method of writing, for it always represents the same sounds. Of course the means exist in the alphabet for writing out the syllable in full, if preferred.

TABLE OF THE *ƩN*-HOOK.

pʃn	tʃn	çʃn	kʃn
bʃn	dʃn	jʃn	gʃn
fʃn	ŧʃn	sʃn	ʃ-ʃn
vʃn	đʃn	zʃn	ʒʃn
	rʃn	lʃn	
mʃn	nʃn	ŋʃn	hʃn

94. On the straight strokes, the *ʃn*-hook is made on the opposite side from the *n*-hook; and on the curves it is made in the position of the *n*-hook, but double its size, as illustrated above.

95. The most general use of this hook is at the termination of words; as *opʃun*, *pɷrʃun*. If a vowel follow the stroke on which the hook is written, it is read between the stroke and the hook; as *evaʒun*, *relaʃun*, *adɷraʃun* *konsiduraʃun*. m

96. The *ʃn*-hook is often conveniently used in the middle of a word also; thus, *dikʃunari*, *revɷlyʃunari*.

97. The *s*-circle may be added by writing it distinctly on the inside of these hooks, to the straight strokes as well as the curves; thus, *kondiʃunz*, *invaʒunz*.

98. Word-signs.— *objekʃun*, *subjekʃun*, *okaʒun*.

READING EXERCISE XXVII.

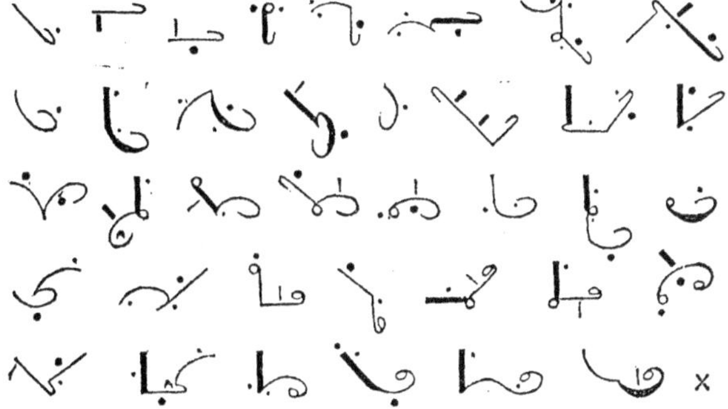

WRITING EXERCISE XXVIII.

Pɷʃun, stɑʃun, kompaʃun, ambiʃun, kondiʃun, nɛgɑʃun, komyꝏnikaʃun, dɥrɑʃun, pɛtiʃun, indikɑʃun, fɥʒun, invɑʒun, ilɥʒun, revɷlɥʃun, konsɷlɑʃun, ɛmɷʃun, admiʃun, nɑʃun, am-yɯniʃun. Prɷfɥʒun, refɵrmɑʃun, sɛlekʃun, delɛgɑʃun, dɛprȷ-vɑʃun, sɥpurviʒun, kɷhɛʒun.

Pɛtiʃunur, eksɛkɥʃunur, okɑʒunal, revɷluʃunɑri. Paʃunz, ɛdiʃunz, viʒunz, ɛfɥʒunz, miʃunz, nɷʃunz, administrɑʃunz.

---

99. Vowel Contractions.—The vowels being so simply and easily formed, but little is to be desired in the way of abbreviating the method of writing them; but as considerable time is lost by lifting the pen in passing from one to another, it is no small advantage to write two vowel sounds

in one sign, where it can be done without ambiguity. Such a contraction is quite common in words where the short vowel *i* immediately precedes another of the simple vowels; as in the words *varius, efluvia, enunʃiaʃun, rafiɷ:* becoming nearly like *varyus, efluvya, enunʃyaʃun, rafyɷ.* This coalition of vowels so nearly produces the articulations *ya, yə, yɷ, yu,* that the signs for these improper diphthongs are used in such cases; thus, *varius,* *asɷʃiaʃun,* *rafiɷ.*

100. Dissyllabic Diphthongs.—The following is an additional scale of diphthongs, simply formed, and some of which are very useful:—
ei ai ɑi oi ɷi ɯi; as in *klai,* *snɷi,* *ɷiy* *stɷik,* *lɯi.* The sign for *ɷi* may also be used for *ɷe* in a few words that would otherwise be inconveniently written; as *hwensɷevur, hwarsɷevur, lɷest, &c.*

101. The close diphthong heard in the word *aye,* though differing but little from either *i* or *ɑi,* is written thus,

READING EXERCISE XXVIII.

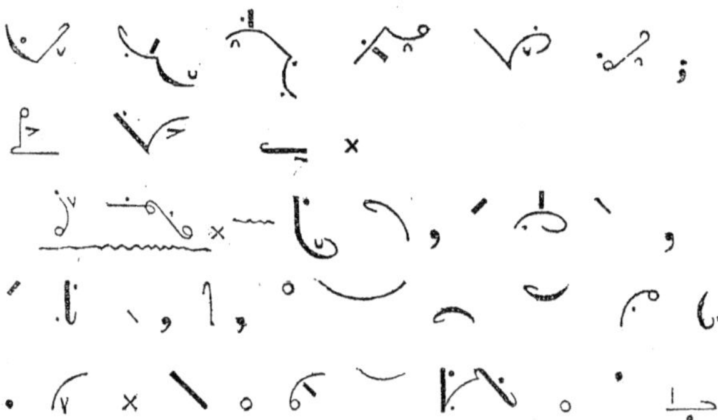

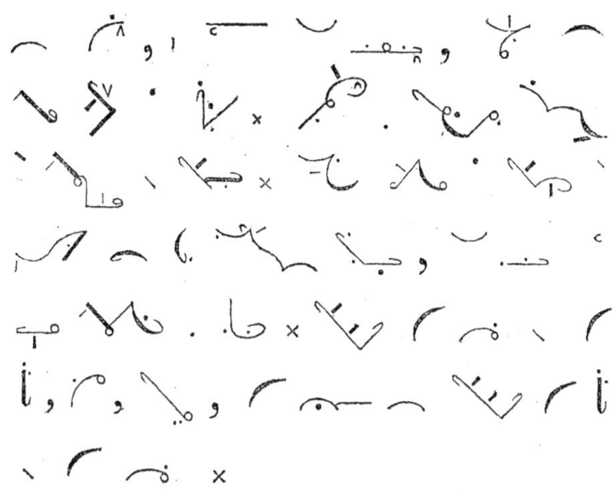

WRITING EXERCISE XXIX.

Envius, erωnius, vεriaʃun εnunʃiaʃun, glωrius, sεrius, paliaʃun, alεviaʃun, hωmiopaŧi.

Klai, flei, bilωi, stωikal, lωest, glɯi.

Ambiʃun iz đε okaʒun ov sεdiʃun, konfɥʒun, and desωlaʃun, and arʊzez evuri εvil εmωʃun and paʃun.

An qs, pikiŋ up a lįunz skin hwiç had bin ŧrωn awa, pɯt it on; and runiŋ intɯ đε wɯdz and pastyurz, bεgan to bra, in imitaʃun ov đε lįunz rωr, hwiç trɯ đε floks intɯ teribel kωnfɥʒun. At leŋŧ đε ωnur kam aloŋ and wɯd hav bin struk wiđ konsturnaʃun else, but upon hiz lisniŋ mωr klωsli, hε sɯn se đε ilɥʒun in đε vʊs, and so, mωrωvur, đε qsez εrz stikiŋ ʊt. Wiđ nω hezitaʃun hε ran up tɯ đε qs and wiđ hiz kujel bεt him sεverli, saiŋ: "Yɯ fɯl, yɯ hav bin đε okaʒun ov skariŋ đε floks, but į'l hav yɯ tɯ nω elđω yω lɯk lįk a lįun, yet yɯ bra lįk an qs.

Aplikaʃun.—Afektaʃun wil ʃɯrli ekspωz a man tɯ derįʒun in prωpωrʃun tɯ hiz asumpʃun.

Review.—(94.) On which side of the straight strokes is the *ʃn*-hook made? How is it made to the curves? (95.) How is the *ʃn*-hook read? (96.) Give new examples of the two situations in which it may be used. (97.) How is the *s*-circle added? (98.) What are the word signs? (99.) Explain the vowel contractions. (100.) The dissyllabic diphthongs. (101.) How is *aye* written?

LESSON X.

HALF-LENGTH STROKES.

102. In consequence of the frequent recurrence of the sounds *t* and *d*, it is found very convenient to give them another and more contracted representation; it is also rendered necessary by the fact that one frequently follows the other, and since they are both perpendicular signs their repetition at full length would carry the writing too far below the line for convenience.

103. But every philosophical means has already been resorted to for the purpose of giving to Phonography the ultimatum of brevity; and if the following scheme has only the semblance of philosophy in it, it will be as much as can be expected. In chemistry, it is well known, the more a substance—a poison, or steam, for instance—is concentrated, the greater is its power: so, in order to get a repetition of the consonants *t* and *d* without writing them at length, the single strokes | and |, by being compressed into *half their length*, are made to represent the addition of a *t* and *d*. And the principle is extended, by license, to the other consonants.

104. The strokes *y*, *y*, *w*, *h*, are not made half-length for the addition of *t* and *d*.

105. To illustrate this principle, suppose the word *faded* is to be written: there are three consonants in it, all downward strokes, which would carry the last *d* the length of two strokes below the line; but by making the first *d* half its usual length, another *d* is supposed to be added, and the word is thus neatly written: *faded.*

The principle is further illustrated by the following words: *tok*, *tokt*; *rap*, *rapt*; *liv*, *livd*.

106. A vowel before a half-length consonant is read before both letters; as *apt*, *est*, *qrt*, *akt*; but when placed after, it is read immediately after the primary letter, and the added *t* or *d* follows it; thus, *kot*, *rot*, *spit*, *kontemt*, *litel*.

107. As a general thing the light strokes, when halved, are followed by the light sound, *t*, and the heavy ones by the heavy sound, *d*; thus, *tot*, *gift*, *yuzd*, *fot*. This is always the case where no vowel intervenes between the sound of the stroke and the *t* or *d* expressed by the halving, as in the above words. But under other circumstances a heavy consonant sound often follows a light one, and vice versa; and in such cases the half-length light strokes must express the addition of *d*, and the heavy ones that of *t*; as *melted*, *pepeld*, *alfabet*.

108. Since, however, the heavy strokes occupying the places of *r*, *l*, *m*, and *n*, are not made half-length, these four letters, when followed by a *d*, are, for the sake of distinction, made heavy; as *gerd*, *old*, *formd*; and light when a *t* follows; as *qrt*, *delit*, *remit*. The *l* is struck upward when *t* is to be added, and when *d*, downward, since in this direction it is more easy to make a heavy stroke.

109. A stroke beginning or ending with the *s* circle, or either of the hooks, or both hook and circle, is also made half-length, when necessary; thus, *sped*, *swift*, *tret*, *komplet*, *frat*, *strat*, *seteld*; *bedz*, *mats*, *band*, *pafent*, *plant*, *grand*; the order of reading being the same as in the full length strokes.

110. It must be observed that when the circle *s* is written to a half-length consonant it must be read after the added *t* or *d*; because the *s* is added to the consonant after it has been halved; thus, *pat*, *pats*, (not *past*,) *fat*, *fats*, (not *fast*.)

111. Half-length consonants, unconnected with other strokes, should be employed only for words containing but one vowel; as *vod*, *nit*; and the two full length letters should be used in words containing two or more vowels; as *avod*, *yunit*.

112. The past tense of verbs ending like *part*, are more conveniently written thus, *parted*, than

113. There are a few words in which *t* and *d* occur three times in succession, which make it necessary to separate the half-length from the long stroke; thus, *atitud*.

114. Since the half-lengths occupy only a portion of the usual space, they follow the rules given to the horizontals, of accented vowel positions, *above* or *on* the line according as the consonant has a first place, or a second or third-place vowel; thus, *stret*, *spred*, *find*, *fend*.

READING EXERCISE XXIX.

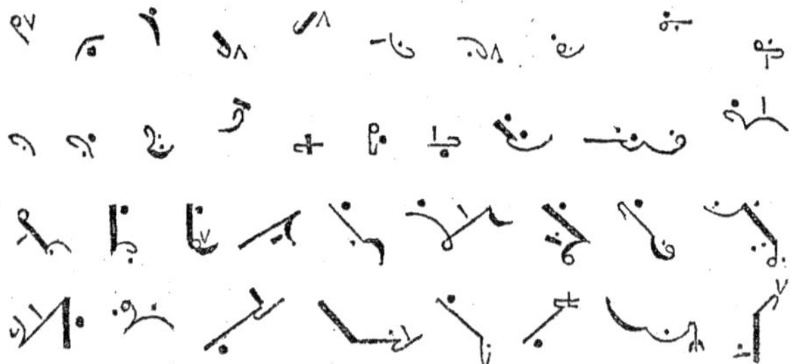

WRITING EXERCISE XXX.

Fɛt, fat, ʃɛt, lat, mat, nɷt, spot, skʊt, savd, sɛlt, smi̥t, sɛnt; pɷnt, bend, kontend, ɵrdand, enjɷnd, ki̥nd, rɛfi̥nd, leŋtend, land, mi̥nd; pants, bandz, prɛtendz, kontents, disksunts; frend, advent, hqrdli, survd, konsumd, hɷldz, hɛted, habit, hurld, perild, upri̥t, gqrded, dɛli̥ted, upwurd, pursɛvd, gi̥ld, lektyurd.

---

115. Under certain circumstances *t* and *d* should not be represented by half-length strokes: *First,* When a vowel follows *t* or *d* at the end of a word; thus having *gilt,* we cannot make *gilti* by placing *i* after the half-length *l,* for it would then read *gilit;* hence the stroke *t* must be written in order to give a place after it for the vowel; thus *gilti.* *Second,* In many words of one syllable, where if the vowels were omitted, or indistinct, they would be mistaken for the vowel word-signs; thus, *bad,* instead of ; *put,* instead of . *Third,* When the half-stroke would not make a distinct angle with the preceding or following stroke, as *amend,* instead of ; and in some other cases that will suggest themselves to the learner.

116. HALF-LENGTH WORD-SIGNS.

particular / opportunity	cannot / account	Lord / word
spirit	God / good	immediate-ly / made
told		
toward	great	might
gentlemen / gentleman	after	not / nature
	thought	
quite / could	that / without	went / wont
called	establish-ment	under
according-ly	short	world

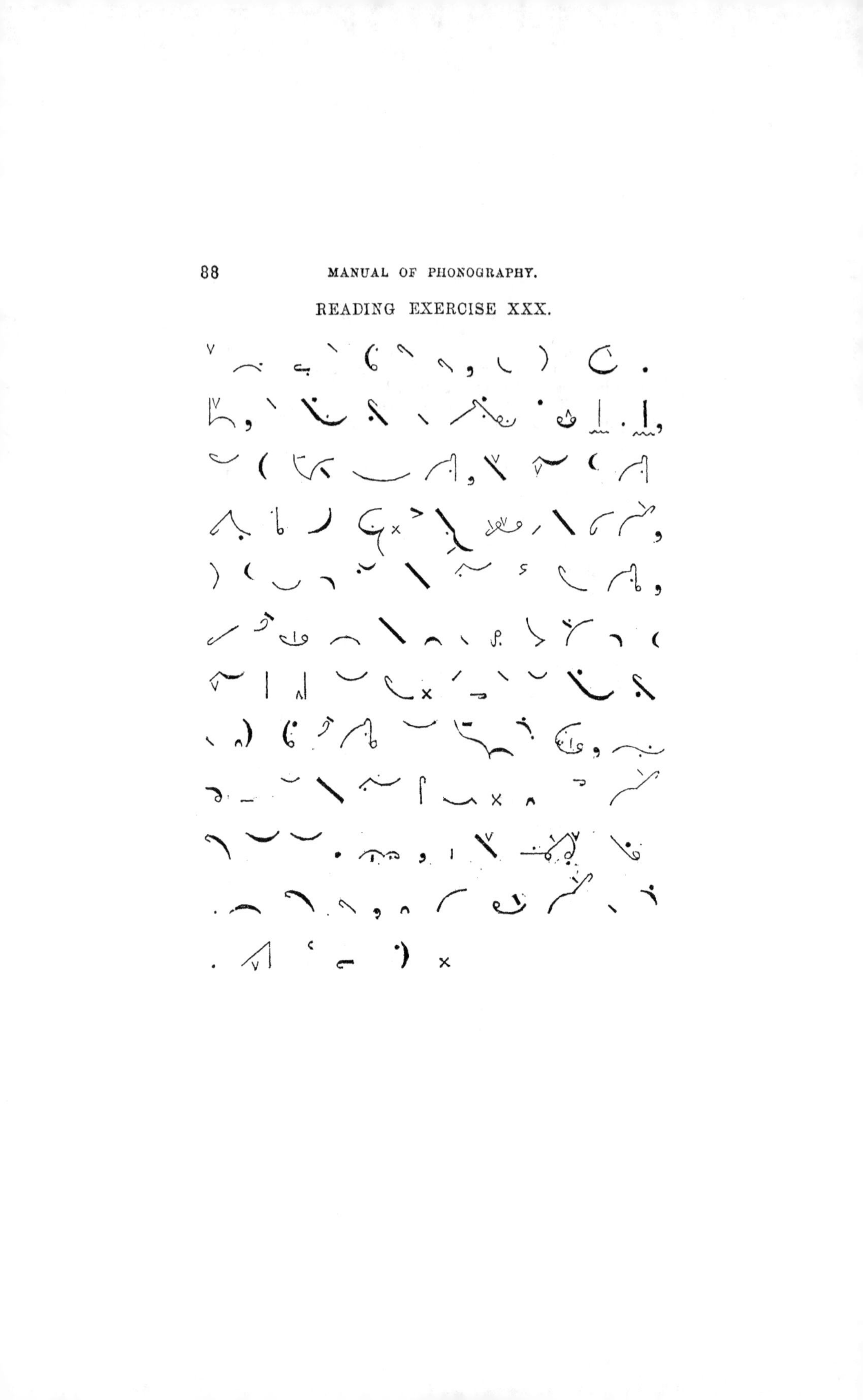

READING EXERCISE XXX.

WRITING EXERCISE XXXI.

LɵRENS LɑZI, ɵR LURNIŊ FꞷNOGRAFI.

Tɯ lurn, ɵr not tɯ lurn, đat iz đɛ kwestyun:
hweđur 'tiz nꞷblur in đɛ mįnd tɯ sufur
đɛ kompleks kwibelz ov ambigyɯus Loŋhand;
ɵr tɯ opꞷz wiđ pen and vɵs ɑ tȣzand erurz,
and, bį opꞷziŋ, end đem?—Tɯ lurn,—tɯ rįt,—
and, bį Fꞷnografi, tɯ sɑ wɛ end
đɛ fɵlsitiz, đɛ tȣzand tɛdyus ilz
Loŋhand prꞷdɥsez—'tiz ɑ konsumɑʃun
dɛvȣtli tɯ bɛ wiʃt. Tɯ rįt;—tɯ lurn;—
tɯ lurn! but đen tɯ wurk;—ɋi, đɋr'z đɛ rub;
fɵr, tɯ akwįr đis ɋrt, hwot tɵl mɑ kum
ɑr į kan ʃufel ɵf mį habits ꞷld,
ʃɯd giv mɛ pɵz: đɑr'z đɛ rɛspekt
đat mɑks Ɵrtografi ov sꞷ loŋ lįf;
fɵr ꞩ hɯ wɯd bɑr đɛ inɥmurabel ilz ov Loŋhand,
its bɋrbarus leŋθ, its ambigɥiti,
its çįld-tɵrmentiŋ difikultiz, and
its wont ov rɯl, tɯgeđur wiđ đɛ tɵl
hwiç pɑʃent skrįbz ov suç ɑ sistem hav,
hwen hɛ himself mįt hiz rɛlɛsment mɑk
wiđ ɑ Duzen Lesunz. ꞩHɯ yet wɯd yɯz
đis bɋrbarus relik ov ȣr bįgon dɑz,
but đat đɛ dred ov sumθiŋ tɯ bɛ lurnt,—
(đat wɛk unmanli ɛz, from hɯz embrɑs
nꞷ lazi man kan got,)—puzelz đɛ wil,
and mɑks him rađur bɑr ɛ'n fɵlsitiz,
đan lurn đɛ trɯθ hɛ yet nꞷz nuθiŋ ov.
Ꝺus indꞷlens tɯ ɵft rɛtɋrdz đɛ mįnd;
and đus đɛ progres ov ɑ yɯsful ɋrt
iz çɛkt, but not prɛvented; fɵr đɛ tįm
wil kum hwen đis sɑm brɛf Fꞷnografi
ʃal trįumf ꞷ'r its fįnal opꞷnent.

REVIEW.—(102.) What is the necessity for a second mode of representing *t* and *d*? (103.) What is their second representation? Explain the philosophy of halving a consonant. (104.) What strokes are not written half-length? (107.) What is the general rule for knowing whether a *t* or a *d* is added? In what case does this rule never fail? (108.) What half-length light strokes are made heavy for the addition of *d*? In what direction are the half-lengths *l* and *r* struck, for the addition of *d*? for the addition of *t*? (109.) May strokes having initial and terminal circles and hooks be halved? (110.) When the circle *s* is written to a half-length sign, is it read before or after the added *t* or *d*? (111.) Should a half-length letter alone be used with two vowels? (113.) How are words written in which *t* and *d* occur three times in succession? (114.) What is the rule for the position of half-length strokes? (115.) What is the first case in which a stroke should not be halved for a following *t* or *d*? The 2nd? the 3rd? (116.) Give the first column of word-signs; the 2nd; the 3rd.

LESSON XI.

SPECIAL CONSONANT CONTRACTIONS.

117. The *s*-circle, initial and final hooks, and half-length stems, are contracted modes of writing that admit of general application, and of perfect vocalization. But as Phonography studies the greatest degree of abbreviation, consistent with legibility, a few combinations of consonants, and some syllables of frequent occurrence, are provided with special forms of contraction, some of which only are capable of vocalization. Of these there are the frequent *st*, in the past participle of verbs ending in *s*, in the superlative of adjectives, and in many other words, as *pressed, wisest, stake*; the *str* in the comparative of adjectives, &c., as *faster, sister;* the initial *instr*, of *instruction*, &c., and the final *s-shn* of some nouns, as *position*; all of which it would often be inconvenient to write in the usual manner. There are also prefixes, derived from the Latin, of frequent occurrence, but of inconvenient length, as *accom-plish, incon-siderate, recom-pense, enter-prise, circum-vent*. The method of writing these contractions constitutes the last lesson proper of the system, and is one that should receive special attention, in order that the somewhat arbitrary mode of writing shall not be forgotten.

There is a kind of principle manifested, however, in most of the contractions, which renders it almost impossible for them to escape the memory, if they be once thoroughly mastered and have been transfixed by the magical influence of practice.

THE LOOPS *ST* AND *STR*.

118. The plan of writing *st* in some shorter way than by the circle *s* and stroke *t*, was devised chiefly for the purpose of still farther obviating the difficulty of words running too far below the line. By simply lengthening the *s*-circle to one-third the length of the stroke on which it occurs, the sound of *t* is aded; thus, *bas*, *bast*, *rɛjɔs*, *rɛjɔst*; *vast*, *prɛst*. In other words, a loop written one-third the length of the consonant to which it is attached, represents the combined sounds of *s* and *t*, with no vowel between them; and by license it may also signify *zd*, as in *klɔzd*.

119. The *s* or *z* may be added for plurals, &c., by striking the loop through the long sign and forming the circle on the opposite side; as *bɛsts*, *gɛsts*, *nɛsts*.

120. This loop may also be written initially; as in the words *stop*, *stat*, *staf*, *stil*, *stɛm*. And it may be used between two strokes, only when written to *t*, *d*, *ç*, *ȷ*; as *testifi*, *distiŋgwiʃ*, *justifi*.

121. When this loop is written in the position of the *r*-hook, like the *s*-circle it takes the additional power of *r*; thus, *stupur* *stikur*; and when turned in the *n*-hook position, it assumes the power of that hook; as *kondenst*, *agɛnst*.

122. Half-length strokes also admit of the *st*-loop, to a limited extent; as *midst*, *stydent*.

123. When a word begins with a vowel, followed by *st* or *zd*, the half-length stroke, and not the loop, must be used; as *histuri*, *wizdum*, *sistem*.

124. By extending the loop to two-thirds the length of the stroke, *r* is added; as in the words *Webstur*, *sistur*, *mastur*. This loop should not be used initially

It may be turned on the *n*-hook side of the stroke to express *nstr*; as *punstur*, and the circle *s* may be used as with the *st* loop; thus, *festurz*, *masturz*.

125. Word Sign.—The *st*-loop is used as a word-sign for *first*, written on the line and inclined to the right, thus, *o*

READING EXERCISE XXXI.

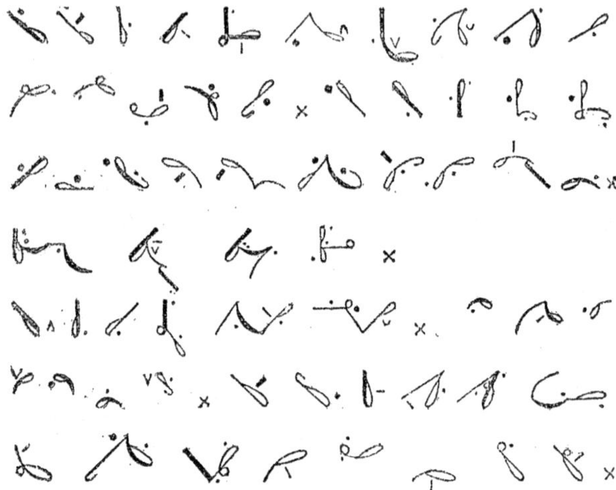

WRITING EXERCISE XXXII.

Pɑst, bωst, dust, tɑst, ɡest, kost, gust, fɛst, sɑfest, rωst, arest, arʊzd, rust, lɛst, last, mist, mωst, amɥzd, fɪnest, dɛnʊnst; stɯp, stedfast, stɑgnant, stif, stωv, stɛr, stil, stem; stopur, stɑjur, stagur; distiŋktli, justifikɑʃun; bɛsts, bωsts, kasts, rɛzists, iɔfests, mɑsts; stilt, stɯrd, stɑrd, stamt; kondenst, agenst. Bωstur, blustur, fastur, blistur, sistur, impostur; punstur, spinsturz. Stɑted, advanst, suprest, prɛtekst, prωdɥst.

READING EXERCISE XXXII.

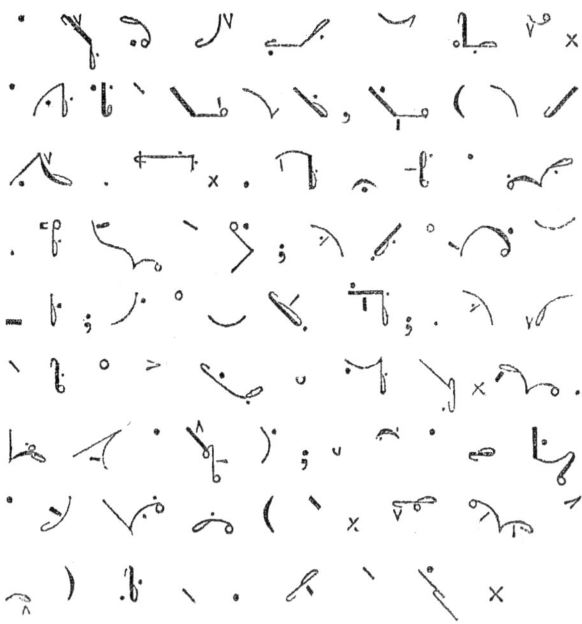

WRITING EXERCISE XXXIII.

LUV.—Polok.

Hal, hωli luv! ƌɤ wurd ƌat sumz ɵl blis,
givst and rɛsɛvst ɵl blis, fulest hwen mωst
ƌɤ givst! spriŋ-hed of ɵl ɤr hapines,
dɛpest hwen mωst iz drɵn! emblem ov God!
ωrflωiŋ mωst hwen grɑtest numburz driŋk;
entįrli blest, bɛkɵz ƌɤ sɛkst nω mωr,
hωpst not, nɵr fɛrst, but on ƌɛ prezent livst,
and hωldst purfekʃun smįliŋ in ƌįn ɑrmz.
Dizurnur ov ƌɛ rįpest graps ov jơ,
ʃɛ gaƌureƋ and sɛlekteƋ wiƌ hur hand

el fįnest relifez, el farest sįts,
el rarest odurz, el divįnest sundz,
el tets, el feliŋz derest tu de sol,
and briŋz de holi mikstyur hom, and filz
de hqrt wid el supurlativz ov blis.

ANOMALOUS *N* AND *ΣN*.

126. When the sounds *spr*, *str*, and *skr* follow *n* in such words as *inspirafun*, *instrukt*, *inskrįb*, it is impossible, with the use heretofore made of *n*, to write the circle *sr* to the strokes *p*, *t*, *k*, without making it on the back of the *n*, thus, which is difficult to do, and unseemly when done. To obviate this difficulty the stroke is permitted, in these cases, to be struck backward or vertically, as the nature of the case may require; but, as there is never occasion for any vowel but the first-place *i*, the stroke for the *n* need not be written full length; indeed, it may be regarded as the *n* hook used initially; thus, *instrukfun*, *insupurabel*, *inskripfun*.

127. In a considerable class of words the syllable *fun* follows after the sound of *s* or *z*, as *pozifun*, *desizun*, &c., which would require that the strokes for these sounds, with the *fun* hook appended, be employed; but such would be inconvenient forms, and hence it is allowable to use the circle and turn a hook for *fun* on the opposite side of the stroke; thus, *desizun*, *supozifun;* the same license is allowed for the loops *st* and *str*, thus, *molestafun*, *ilustrafun*. This hook is used in some such words as *purswazun;* and it may also be used when followed by the termination *al;* as, *pozifunal.*

128. If it be required to write the syllable *fun* after *ns*, the circle for the latter combination may be employed, and

the hook turned on the opposite side ; thus, *compensa-ʃun*. The plural may be formed, in all these cases, by adding the circle to the *ʃn*-hook ; thus, *sųpurstiʃunz*, *kondensɑʃunz*.

READING EXERCISE XXXIII.

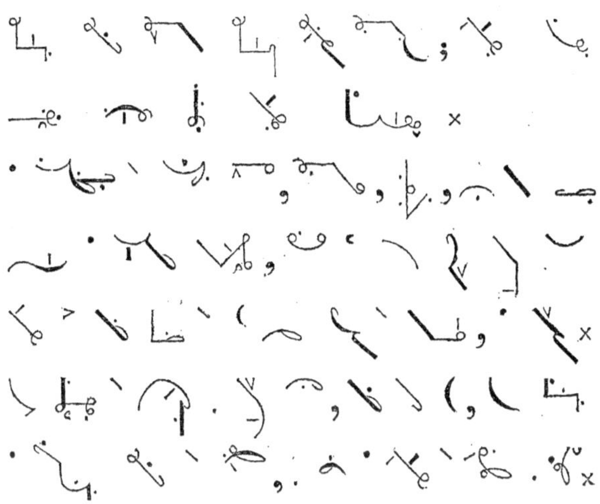

WRITING EXERCISE XXXIV.

Insųpurabli, instrukt, instrɯment, instrɯmentaliti, inskrįbd, inskrɯtabel ; pɷziʃun, desiʒun, kεzɑʃun, sivilizɑʃun, mųziʃan ; manifestɑʃun, inkrustɑʃun, kondensɑʃun, dispensɑʃun ; sup-ɷziʃunz, akųzɑʃunz, ilustrɑʃunz, sensɑʃunz.

Studi kondensɑʃun in yɯr stįl ov kompɷziʃun, fer đɷ it mɑ kost yɯ sum trubel at furst, yet it wil asist yɯ tɯ mastur purspikųiti and presiʒun, on đε akwiziʃun ov hwiɋ, ɋast and pʊurfɯl rįtiŋ iz bæst. Promted bį ɑ dezįr fer đε akwiziʃun ov welđ, man stemz đε stermz ov đε ɷʃan, landz on evuri kɷst, in spįt ov đε grɑtest dɑnjurz arįziŋ from klįmet er đε hand ov unsivilįzd man. Rεlijun folɷz in đε wɑk ov komurs, kontendiŋ agenst its εvilz ; and đus, hwįl savej nɑʃunz ɋr blest wiđ đε lįt ov sivilizɑʃun, đɑ ɋr put in pozeʃun ov đε wurd ov inspirɑʃun, and tet đε egust trɯđz ov đε gospel dispensɑʃun.

REVIEW.—(117.) What are the special consonant contractions? (118.) How are *st* and *zd* written? (119.) How may the circle be added? (120.) In what situations may the loop be written? (121.) When written in the place of the *r*-hook what power does it give the stroke? What, when written in the *n*-hook place? (122.) How should the words *midst* and *student* be written? (123.) In what case is the loop not to be used? (124.) How is *str* written? What effect does it have on this loop to place it on the *n*-hook side? If the sound of *s* follow, how is it wrtten? (125). What is the word-sign in this lesson? (126.) When is it necessary to use the anomalous mode of writing *n*? How is it written? (127.) Under what circumstance is the anomalous *fn* employed? How is it written? (128.) Suppose it be required to write *fn* after *ns*, how is it done? If *s* follow the *fn*, how may it be written?

LESSON XII.

PREFIXES AND OTHER CONTRACTIONS

129. PREFIXES. — The following are some additional prefixes and affixes that are found convenient and suggestive with the advanced phonographer. They should be written near the word, but not joined.

Akom is expressed by a heavy dot, placed before the initial end of the following consonant; thus, *akumpani*, *akomplis*.

Surkum, by a small circle placed in the first vowel position of the next consonant; as, *surkumstans*, *surkumskrib*.

Dekom, by | as, *dekompozifun*.

Diskom, diskon, by as, *diskonsurted*.

Inkom, inkon, by written above the other part of the word; as, *inkomplet*, *inkonsistent*.

Intur, intro, by in any position near the following letter; as, *inturvu*, *introdukfun*. By some kind of license, the frequent word *inturest*, is allowed to be written thus: the prefix *intur* being united with the stroke *st*.

Irrekon, by as, *irrekonsilabel*.

Magna, magni, by written above the after part of the word; as, *magnanimus*, *magnifi*.

Rekog, by / as, *rekogniz*.

Rekom, rekon, by as, *rekomend*, *rekonsilabel*.

Self, by a circle at the middle place of the next consonant; as, *selfif*.

Unkom, unkon, by written on the line; as *unkomun,* *unkondiʃunal.*

It is allowable to represent a prefix which is *similar* in sound to one of the foregoing, by one of the signs there furnished; thus, may represent *entur,* as well as *intur;* and may represent *enkum, inkum,* as well as *inkom, inkon.*

130. AFFIXES.—The following affixes are written near the preceding part of the word:—

Biliti, by as, *dyrabiliti,* *probabiliti.*

Li, by written after the word; thus, *paʃentli,* *konstantli.* But where it can be written on without lifting the pen, it is better to do so; thus, *abundantli.*

Ment, by as, *atonment,* *kontentment.* But it may often be written without disconnecting it from the body of the word.

Self, by a circle, as, *miself.* *Selvz,* by making the circle double size; as, *ðemselvz,* *yurselvz.*

Σip, by as, *lordʃip.*

131. A word-sign may be used as a prefix or an affix; as, *advantajus,* *heraftur.*

READING EXERCISE XXXIV.

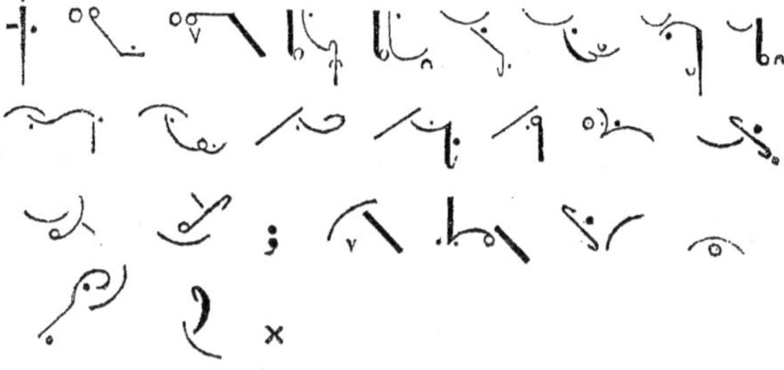

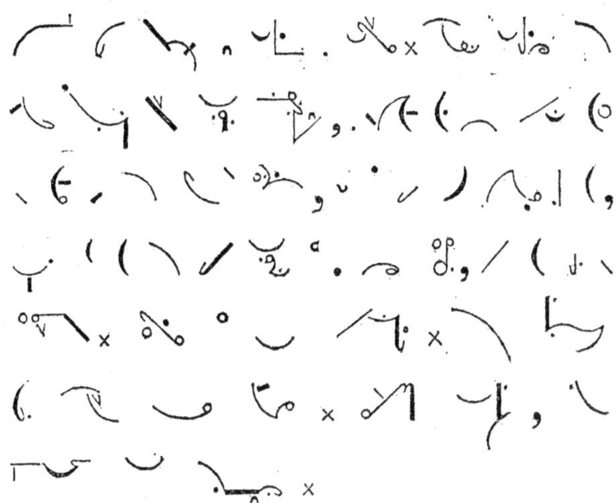

WRITING EXERCISE XXXV.

Akompliʃment, akomωdɑʃun, surkumfleks, surkumnavigɑt, dɛkompωz, diskontinyɯd, inkompatibel, inkonsωlabel, inturupʃun, introdųs, magnifisent, rekogniʃun, rekonsiliɑʃun, self-aʃųrans, unkompromįziŋ, posibiliti, konsɛkwentli, himself, hɵrsmanʃip, đɑrfωr, displeʒur.

Lurn tɯ akomωdɑt yɯrself tɯ surkumstansez. Surkumstanʃal evidens ʃɯd bɛ kɵʃusli enturtɑnd agenst hųman lįf. Bɛ surkumspekt in ɵl yɯr wɑz. It iz unkonfɵrmabel tɯ trɯϑ tɯ sɑ đat kompaʃun, frendʃip, &s., ɑr at botum ωnli selfiʃnes in disgįz; bɛkɵz it iz wɛ ɤrselvz hɯ fɛl pleʒur ɵr pɑn in đɛ gɯd ɵr ɛvil ov uđurz; fɵr đɛ mɛniŋ ov self-luv iz, not đat it iz į đat luvz, but đat į luv mįself.

If đɛ urϑ bɛ surkumskrįbd at đɛ ɛkwɑtur, wɛ obtɑn its grɑtest surkumfurens, hwiɋ iz abɤt 24,780 mįlz; ɑ magnitųd hwiɋ wɛ kan not turm inkonsɛvabel, ɵlđω wɛ mɑ not enturtɑn ɑ veri distiŋkt įdɛa ov it, muɋ mωr wɯd đɛ savej bɛ unkonʃus ov đɛ fakt and unkonvinst, in spįt ov yɯr endevurz tɯ prɯv it. Fɵr unles tanjibel prɯf akumpani đɛ asurʃun, yɯ kan not akompliʃ yɯr ɑm, and suɋ prɯf iz unkontrωvurtibli imposibel.

131. NOMINAL CONSONANT.—It is sometimes necessary to express one or more vowels or diphthongs without a consonant. In this case , may be employed as outlines having no specific values, to which the vowels may be placed; thus, for *Edward* or *Edmund* *A* for *Alfred*, *Eah*, an Irish family surname, &c. The stroke-vowels may be struck *through* the nominal consonant, as *O* for *Oliver*, *U*. Proper names should be written in full when they are known.

132. STROKE *H*.—The stroke-*h* is generally used when it is initial, and is followed by *s*; thus, *hasen;* also when *r* and a vowel, or *r* and some other consonant follow; thus, *huri*, *horizontal* *hurt;* also, in words that contain no other consonant than *hl*, and end in a vowel; thus, *holi*.

133. VOCALIZING THE LARGE CIRCLE.—The large circle *ss* is considered to represent a syllable containing the vowels *i* or *e*, thus, *sis* or *sez*. It may be vocalized to express almost any vowels or diphthongs; as, *purswaziv*.

134. When *p* occurs between *m* and *t*, and *k* between *ŋ* and *ʃ*, (the *p* and *k* being organically inserted in speech, in passing to the next consonant,) these letters may be omitted; thus, *limp*, *limt*, *stamp*, *stamt*, *aŋkʃus*, *distiŋkʃun*.

In cases where *t* comes between *s* and another consonant, the *t* may generally be omitted without detriment to legibility; thus, *mostli*, *restles*, *postpon*, *mistak*.

135. Of The.—The connective phrase "of the," which merely points out that the following noun is in the possessive case, is *intimated* by writing the words between which it occurs *near to each other*, thus showing by their proximity that the one is *of the* other; thus,

luv ov đɛ bytiful, *subjekt ov đɛ wurk.*

Review.—(129.) How is the prefix *accom* written? *Surcum? Decom? Discom, discon? Incom, incon? Inter, intro; interest? Irrecon? Magna, magni? Recog; recom, recon? Self? Uncom, uncon?* How may *enter* be written? *Encum incum?* (130.) How is the affix *bility* written? *ly? ment? self? ship?* What is said about word-signs in this connection? (131.) Explain the nominal consonant. (132.) Under what circumstances is the stroke *h* generally used? (133.) How may the double circle be vocalized? (134.) When may *p* be omitted? *k*, and *t?* (135.) What is said of the phrase *of the?*

LESSON XIII.

UNVOCALIZED WRITING—PHRASEOGRAPHY, &C.

136. As in some of the preceding exercises the manner of writing certain words has been introduced that would not admit of full vocalization, the learner may commence omitting some of the least prominent vowels in his common words. As a general thing these omissions should be the unaccented vowels. But in reporting, no vowels are inserted, except an occasional one that is necessary to distinguish one word from another, where both have the same consonant outline. It requires a good degree of familiarity with the system to be able to read this style of writing readily. After reports are taken, however, it is customary to go over the manuscript and insert the prominent vowels, so that any one may afterward read it with ease.

137. Positive and negative words containing the same consonants, should be distinguished thus:—When the word commences with *r*, (except this letter is followed by *m*,) write the upward *r*; for the positive word, and the downward one for the negative; thus, *responsibel*, *irresponsibel*; *rezolųt*, *irezolųt*. The common words *mortal*, *imortal*, *material*, *imaterial*, may be distinguished by writing the positive on the line, and the negative above it. In all other cases, insert the initial vowel in the negative word, thus; *ilejibel*, &c. The vowel should be inserted first that it may not be omitted in rapid writing.

LIST OF WORDS CONTAINING THE SAME CONSONANTS:

DISTINGUISHED BY A DIFFERENCE OF OUTLINE.

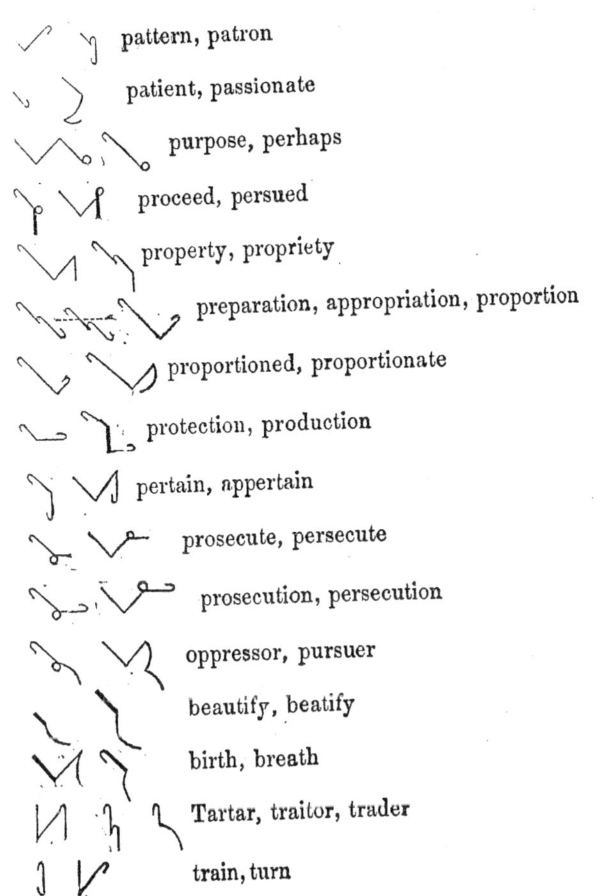

pattern, patron

patient, passionate

purpose, perhaps

proceed, persued

property, propriety

preparation, appropriation, proportion

proportioned, proportionate

protection, production

pertain, appertain

prosecute, persecute

prosecution, persecution

oppressor, pursuer

beautify, beatify

birth, breath

Tartar, traitor, trader

train, turn

attainable, tenable

daughter, debtor, *and* deter

auditor, auditory, editor

diseased, deceased

desolate, dissolute

desolation, dissolution

idleness, dullness

demonstrate, administrate

agent, gentleman

gentle, genteel

cost, caused

collision, coalition, collusion

corporal, corporeal

credence, accordance

greatly, gradually

favored, favorite

fiscal, physical

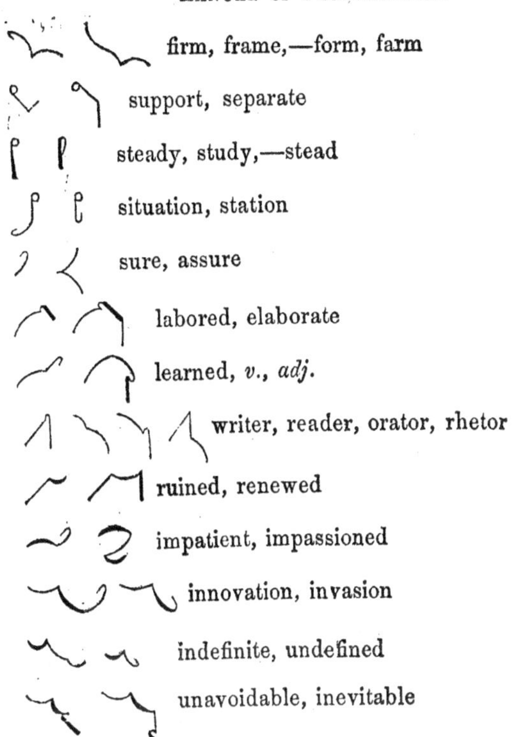

firm, frame,—form, farm

support, separate

steady, study,—stead

situation, station

sure, assure

labored, elaborate

learned, *v.*, *adj.*

writer, reader, orator, rhetor

ruined, renewed

impatient, impassioned

innovation, invasion

indefinite, undefined

unavoidable, inevitable

This list might be greatly extended, but space will not permit it here; from the examples given, the student will learn what forms to give each word, where different outlines are required for words that might be misread, if written alike. Quite an extensive list of words, two or more of them having the same outline, necessarily, are distinguished by position; of which take the following: piety,[1] pity;[2] opposition,[1] position,[2] possesion;[3] prescription,[1] proscription;[2] diminish,[1] admonish,[2] &c.

ALL THE WORD SIGNS ALPHABETICALLY ARRANGED.

*Those marked with a * are written above the line.*

A
all *
already *
an, and
according *
account
advantage
after
again
alone
are
as
be
been
beyond *
but
call *
called *
can
cannot *
care
come
could

dear
difficulty
do
done
establish
every
first
for
from
full
general
gentleman
gentlemen *
give-n *
God *
good
great
have
him
how
I *
immediate *
importance *

improvement
in *
is *
it
kingdom *
language
Lord *
member
might *
more
Mr. *
my *
nature
no
nor *
not *
object
objection
of *
oh
on *
one
opinion *

opportunity	their, there	were
or *	them	where
particular *	then	what *
Phonography	thing *	when *
pleasure	thought *	which
principle	three	while
quite *	to	who
remark *	together	why *
remember	told	will
shall	toward	with *
short *	truth	without
should	two	wont
so	under	word
spirit *	up	world
subject	usual	would
subjection	was	ye *
sure	way	yet
tell, till	we *	you
that *	well	your
the *	went *	yours

On the following page is a different class of word-signs; but two or three new characters are used, the signification being indicated by the position in which the sign is written to the line. Three positions are recognized: on the line, above the line, and through or below the line. In the table the line of writing is suggested by a dotted line, which will guide the learner as to where the word should be written.

Allow
another
any
at
away
by
different-ce
Doctor
down
during
each
either
ever
few
had
happy
here-ar

however
if
itself
kind
large
may
me
mind
much
neither
number
other
ought
our
ours
ourselves
out
own

perfect
practice-able
read
see
than
thank
thee
these
those
though
through
time
us
use (verb)
value
view
will (noun)

CONTRACTED WORDS.

In addition to the word signs that have been given, represented by the alphabetic signs, simple and compound, a list of contracted words is given below. These are abbreviated by giving the more prominent consonants that would be employed in writing the word in full. Words having a * affixed, are written above the line.

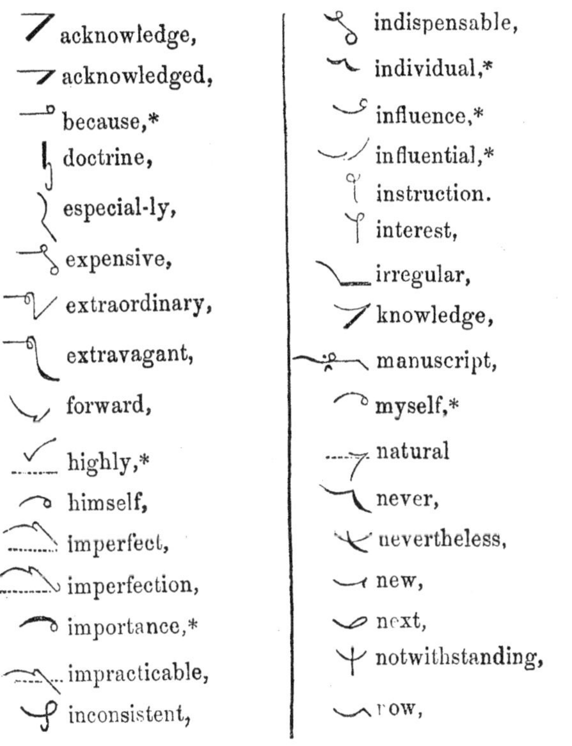

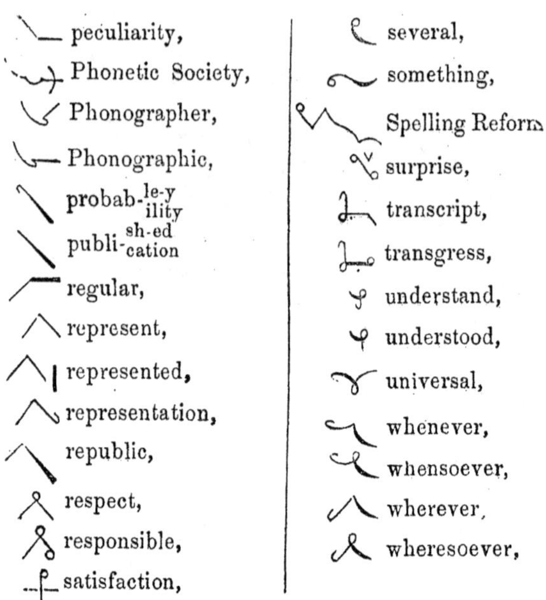

In the complete reporting style, the list of contracted words is considerably extended; but, like the above, they are all very suggestive to the reflective student, and when met with in correspondence or elsewhere, there will seldom be any difficulty in determining what they are. The Reporter's Manual, or other text book of the kind, advertised on the cover, contains complete lists of word-signs, contracted words, phraseography, &c., the study of which will be essential to verbatim reporting, but unnecessary for ordinary purposes of writing.

PHRASEOGRAPHY.

Phraseography consists in writing two or more word signs together, without lifting the pen ; and in the reporting style, it is extended to the writing of word-signs with words written in full, but not vocalized. The first sign in a phrase should be written in its natural position, while those that follow take any position that most faciliates the writing.

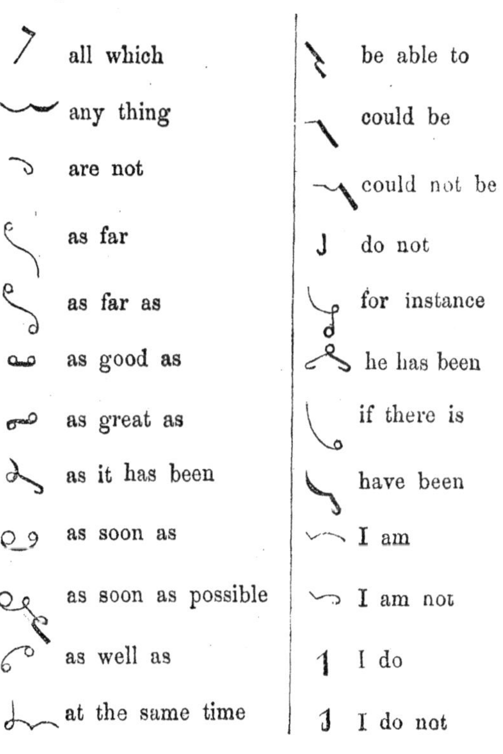

I do not think

I had not

I have

I have been

I have done

I have not

if it

if it had not

if it were

in such

is not

it is

it is not

it would

it would be

I will

I will not

may as well

may be

must be

must have

must not

no doubt

of course

on account of

ought to be

should be

should have

should not

so as to

such as can

that is

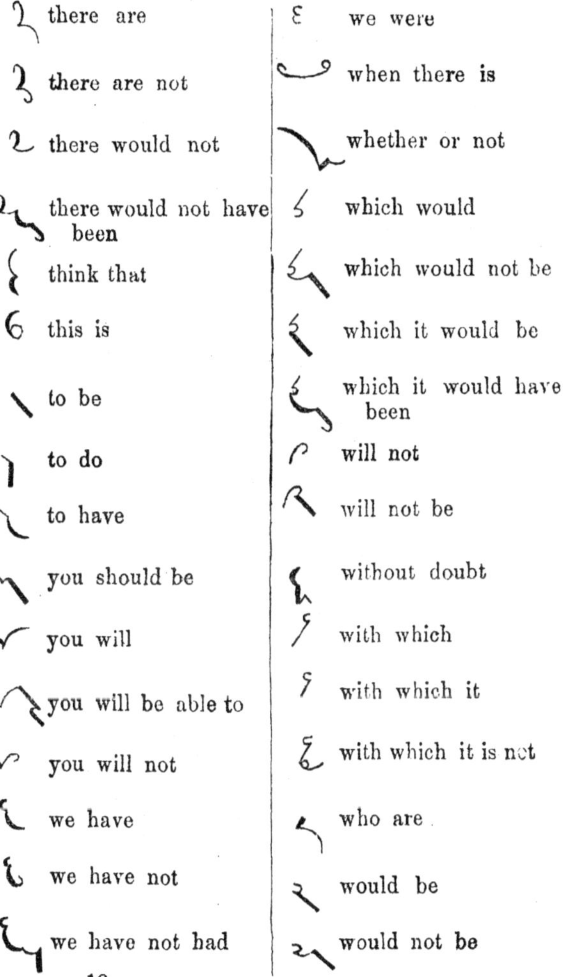

there are

there are not

there would not

there would not have been

think that

this is

to be

to do

to have

you should be

you will

you will be able to

you will not

we have

we have not

we have not had

we were

when there is

whether or not

which would

which would not be

which it would be

which it would have been

will not

will not be

without doubt

with which

with which it

with which it is not

who are

would be

would not be

A word of caution is necessary against a too extensive use of phraseography; it should never be allowed to destroy the lineality of the writing, nor make difficult joinings. In either case, time will be saved by removing the pen from the paper, and commencing afresh.

In phraseography, *the*, or some other unimportant word, is occasionally omitted; as, *in the world*; *for the sake of*. The connective word *and* is sometimes written in connection with the following word, where it may be represented by a short horizontal stroke; *and the, and which.*

WRITING EXERCISE XXXVI.

NOTE.—In the following exercise, instead of repeating the initial words of phrases every time they are to be written, they are indicated by dashes; and the words forming a phrase are connected by hyphens.

Θl. Θl-hiz, (Θl·z) — iz lost, — hwiç, — đis, — đat-iz-sed, — men, —đɑr, — suç-tiŋz, — impertant.

Ov. Ov-it, — hwiç, — suç, — — az-qr, — mɛ, (mj̧,) — mj̧n, (men,) — đɑr, — importans, — hiz, — advantej, — đis kj̧nd, — đat, — đem, — kɷrs.

On. On-əl, — — suç, — akɤnt-ov, — mj̧, — us, — hur, — đɑr, — hiz, — — sj̧d.

Tɯ. Tɯ-it, — dɯ, — bɛ, — hav, — — bin, — — dɯn, — sum-ekstent, — luv, — him, — đat, — meni.

Hɯ. Hɯ-iz-đis, — wɯd, — — not, — mɑ, — — not, (mɑn·t,) — kan, — nɷ, — qr, — — not, (qrn·t.)

Σɯd. Σɯd-bɛ, — not-bɛ, — hav, — dɯ, — not-hav-sed,— — tiŋk-đat.

Ɨ. Ɨ-am, — mɑ, — am-not, or mɑ-not, — dɯ, (had,) — — not, (dɷn·t hadn·t,) — hav, — — not, (wiđ hɯk,) — — — bin — kan-not, — wil, — tiŋk, — ʃal, — nevur, — nɛd, — — not-sɑ, — hɷp, — fɛr, — beg, — am-veri-sori-indɛd, — hɷp-yɯ-wil-not-hav-rɛzun-tɯ-rɛgret, — hav-nɷ-dɤt.

Hɤ. Hɤ-kɯd, — kan, — iz-đis, -- meni, — mɑ, — sɷ-evur.

Yɯ. Yɯ-ʃɯd, — — not, — kɯd, - kan, — mɑ, — wil, — qr, (*r* up stroke) — — not, (qrn·t,) — must, — — bɛ-surten.

Wɛ. Wɛ-wer, — dɯ, — did, — hav, — — sɛn, — ŧiŋk, — ʃal, — qr, (r up strɷk,) — — not, — fįnd.

Wiđ. Wiđ-it, — hwiç, — đis, — đat, — đem, — hwiç-yɯ-qr-akwanted, — suç-az-qr.

Wer. Wer-đa, — wɛ, — đat. Hwar-iz, (hwar'z) (r up strɷk.)

Hwot. Hwot-iz, — wer, — wɯd, — dɯ, — if, — qr, — kɯd-bɛ, — — posibli.

Wɯd. Wɯd-yɯ, — bɛ, — dɯ, — hav, — not, — not-hav-sed.

B. Bɛ-sed, — abel-tɯ. Bį-đis, — mɛ, — meni, — sum-menz, — evuri-menz, — sum-pursunz, — đar.

T. It-iz, — — not, — — sed, — — sɯn, (đɛ last tɯ wiđ a dubel surkel,) — — mį, — ma, — kan, — kɯd, — wɯd. Θt-tɯ-bɛ, At-suç, — prezent, — đɛ-sam-tįm.

D. Dɯ-đa, — not, (dɷn't,) — — dɤt.

Ꞓ. Hwiç-wɯd, — had, — kɯd, — kan, — haz, — — bin, — iz-not, — qr, — — not, — ma, — mįt, — wil, (çl.) Hwiç-it-iz, — — ma, — — wɯd, — — kɯd-not-hav.

F. If-đat, — yɯ, — đar, (dubel-f abuv đɛ lįn.) Fɵr-suç, — — az-qr, — hwiç, — sum-tįm, — fɵr-đar, (dubel-f on đɛ lįn.) If-it-wer — — bɛ — — iz, — — had.

V. Hav-yɯ, — bin, — had, — sed. Veri-gɯd, — grat, — sam, — surten, — wel, — sɯn, — muç. Evuri-pqrt, — wun, — pursun, — man.

Ŧ. Ŧiŋk-đat, — yɯ-qr, — — wil, — — ma.

Đ. Wiđɤt-dɤt, — hwiç, — suç. Đat-it, — — iz, — — haz-bin, — — woz, — qr, — — not, — iz-not. — — tɯ-bɛ, — haz, — hwiç. Đa-wer, — dɯ, — had, — hav, — ma.— Đis-tįm, — da, — advantej. Đar-wɯd, — kan, — kɯd, — — not-hav-bin, — iz, (haz,) — ʃal, — wil, — qr, — — sum-pursunz, — ma.

S. Sɷ-az, — — tɯ, — it-sɛmz, — veri, — litel, — muç, — meni. Suç-wɯd, — iz, — az, — — qr, — — ma, — — kan, — — kɯd, — — hav, — — woz, — — wil.

Z. Iz-it, — — not; az-it, — — wɯd, — — woz, — — ma, — — haz. Az-gɯd, — — az, — grat, — — az, — fqr, — — az, — wel, — meni, — sɯn-az. Iz-not; haz-not.

Σ. Σal-bɛ, — hav, — dɯ, — fįnd, — not, ʃɵrt-hand.

L. Wil, — not, — bɛ, — hav, — fįnd.

R. Ar-yɯ, — sumtįmz, — sori, — not; yɯ qr veri, — — trɯli.

M. Ma-bɛ, — hav, — đa, — az-wel, — konsidur. Mįt-hav, — đis, — sɛm. Must-bɛ, — trį, — dɯ, — kum, — gɷ,

— se, — not. Mœst-hapi, (mœs'-hapi,) — lɪkli, — impertant. Meni-tɪmz, — ŧiŋz, — mœr, — ov-đem.

N. In-el, — konsekwens, — fakt, — đis, — suç, — meniŧiŋz, — hiz. Eni-wun, — θiŋ, — bodi. Nœ-pqrt, — dɤt, — rezun, — mœr, — — tɪm, — wun, — ŧiŋ, (in ful.) Nɤ-sur. Not, — be, — kwɪt, — đat, — in, — œnli, — nɤ,— nœn; nednot. Ner-wer, — iz-đis, — qr.

WRITING EXERCISE XXXVII.

(In phraseography, and containing all the Word-Signs.)

ON IMPRƜVMENT.

Establiʃments fer imprɯvment, pqrtikyɯlurli ov đe mɪnd, qr veri impertant ŧiŋz in a kiŋdum; and đe mœr sœ hwar it-iz yɯʒɯal wiđ-đem tɯ establiʃ and praktis gud prinsipelz. Ɑ fœnœgrafik establiʃment in pqrtikyulur, iz not-œnli an imediet advantej tɯ evuri jentelman hɯ iz a membur ov-it, but tɯ el. Akerdiŋ tɯ jenural œpinyun, Fœnografi iz a subjekt we ʃud elhav pleʒur in, and ŧiŋk upon; wiđɤt it, laŋgwej iz not hwot-itʃud-be—a remqrk in-hwiç-đar-iz grat trɯŧ, and tɯ-hwiç đarkan-be nœ objekʃun. ꟸHɤ, er-on hwot prinsipel, kan we be gud er grat wiđɤt-imprɯvment. Remembur, đat evuri ŧiŋ iz an objekt ov-impertans đat kümz undur it; and, beyond el, đat đe ʃɯr wurd ov đe Lerd God woz given fer imprɯvment.

Aftur hwot-ɪ-hav-tœld-yɯ, ꟸqr-đar yet objekʃunz tɯ-it. Wer đar, an akɤnt ov-đem wud elredi hav-bin given. Grat and gud ŧiŋz kan not kum tɯgeđur wiđɤt-imprɯvment. Σud ɪ-be-tœld-đat it-ma-hav-bin sœ, ɪ-ʃal remqrk-đat, from hwot ɪ nœ ov-đe jenural spirit ov el, đe trɯŧ iz az ɪ-hav given it, ner kan yɯ objekt tɯ-it. In ʃert, jentelmen, establiʃ it az yɯr furst prinsipel, đat-yɯ-wil-not giv up; but, az yɯ hav opurtɥniti, dɯ el đat-kan-be-dun tœrdz imprɯvment in evuri ŧiŋ; sœ wil yɯ giv pleʒur, not tɯ-me-alœn, but tɯ el.

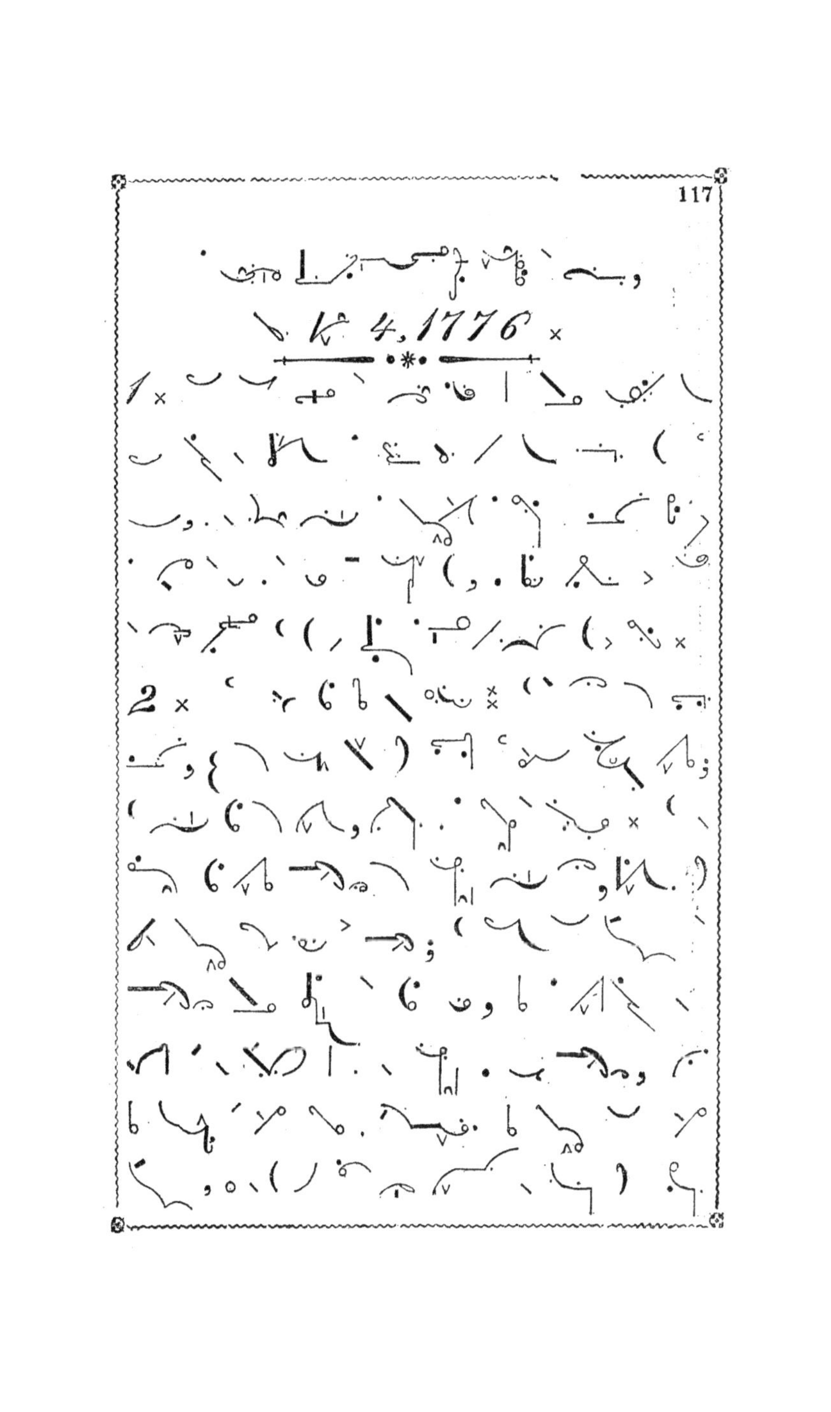
4, 1776
1
2

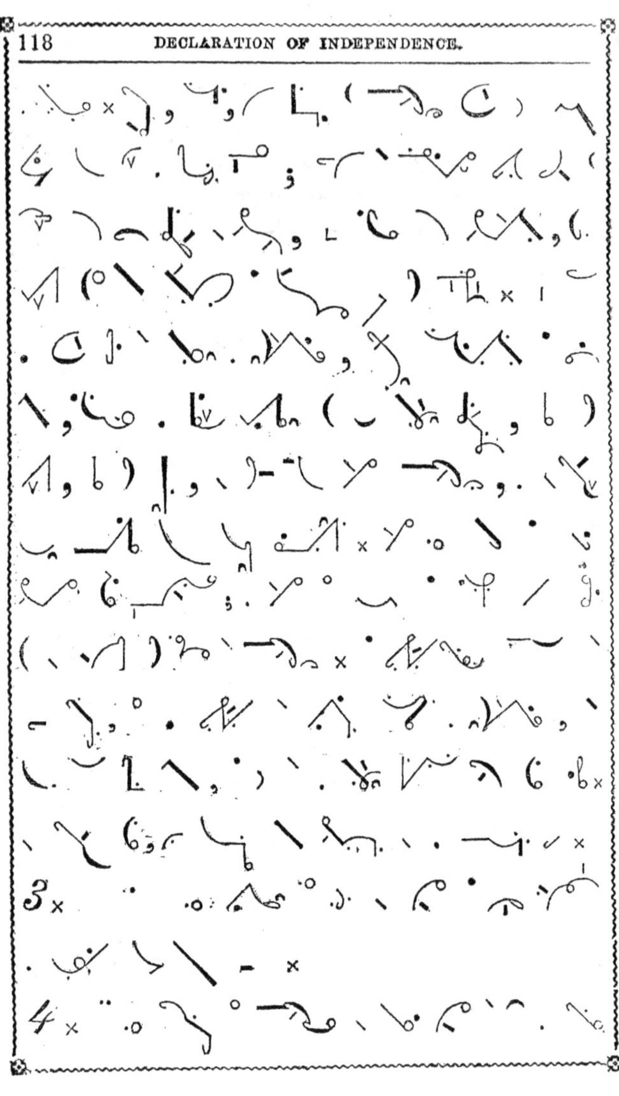

3

4

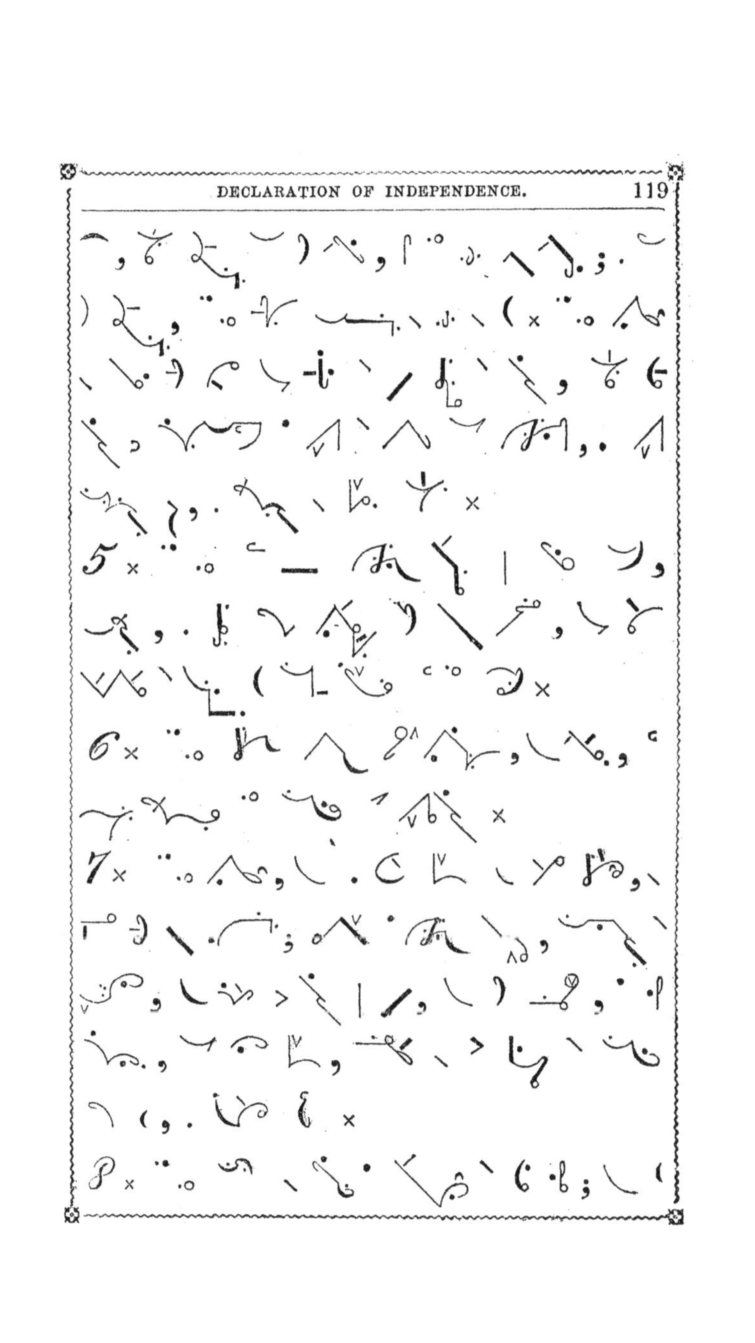

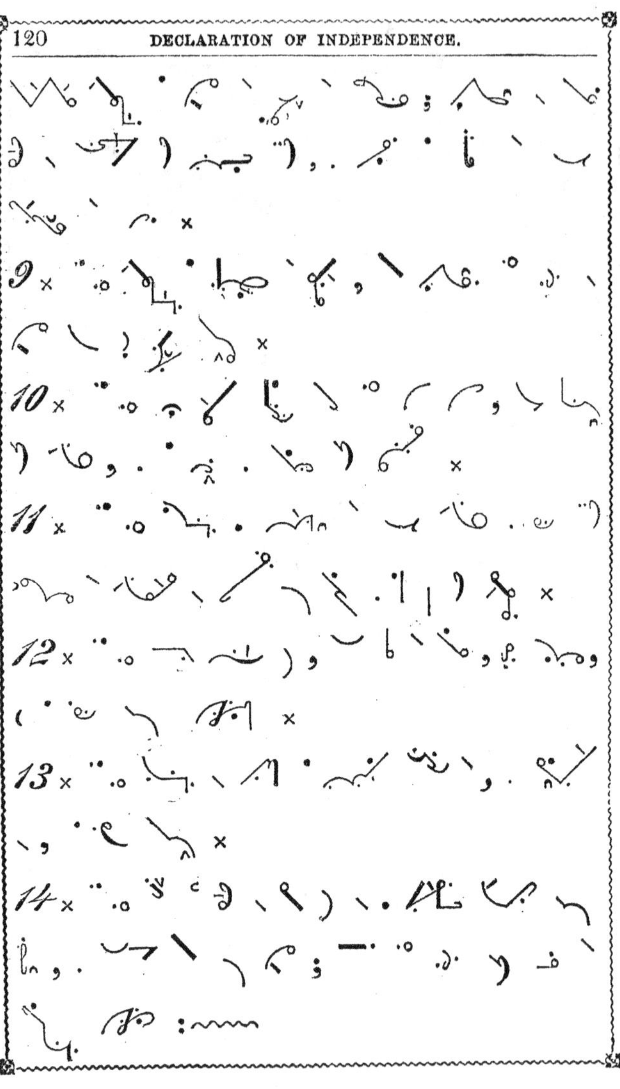
9
10
11
12
13
14

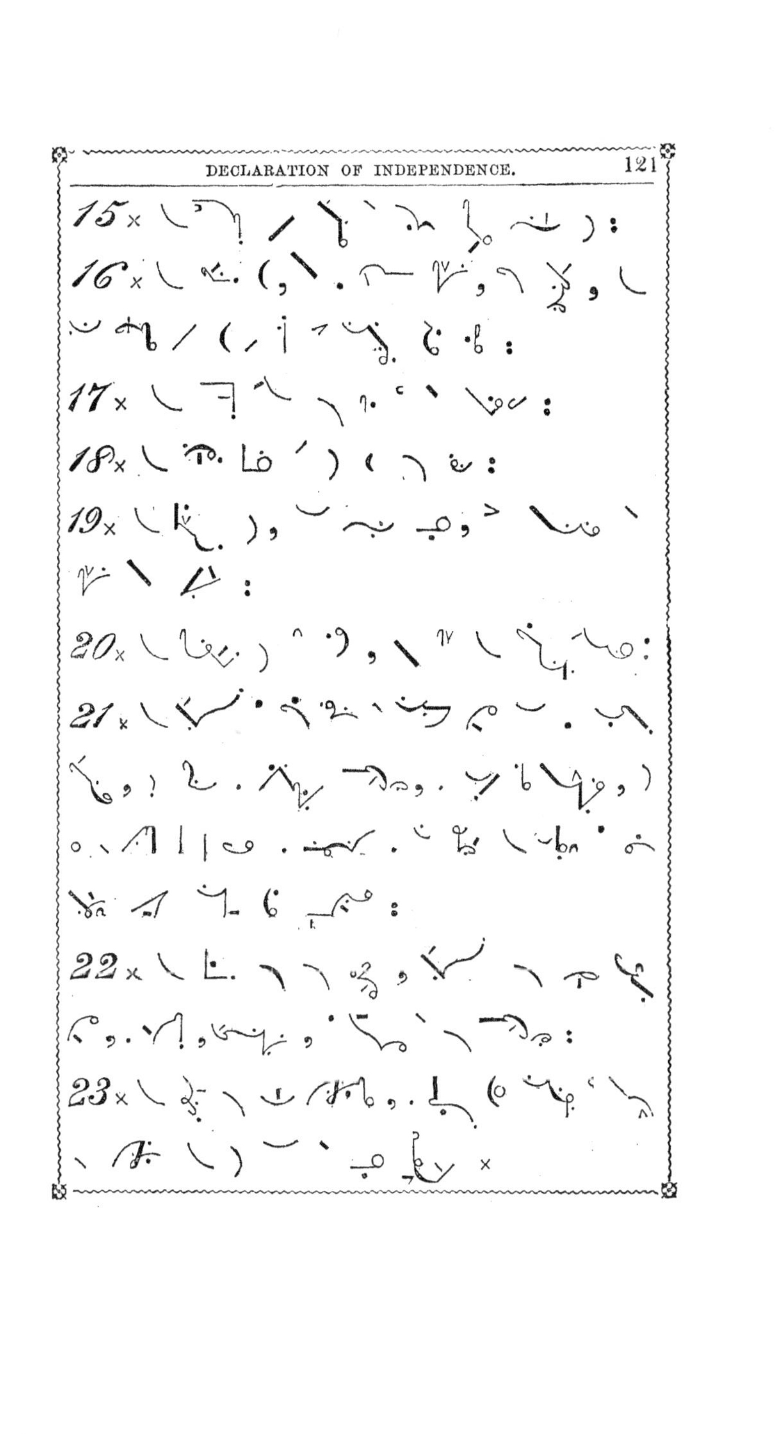

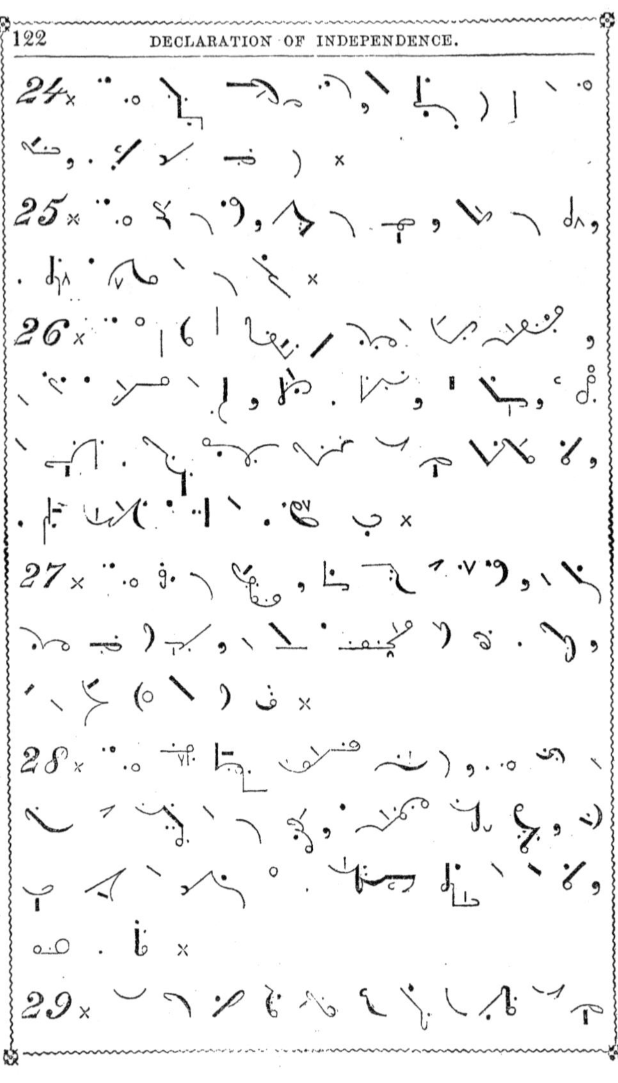

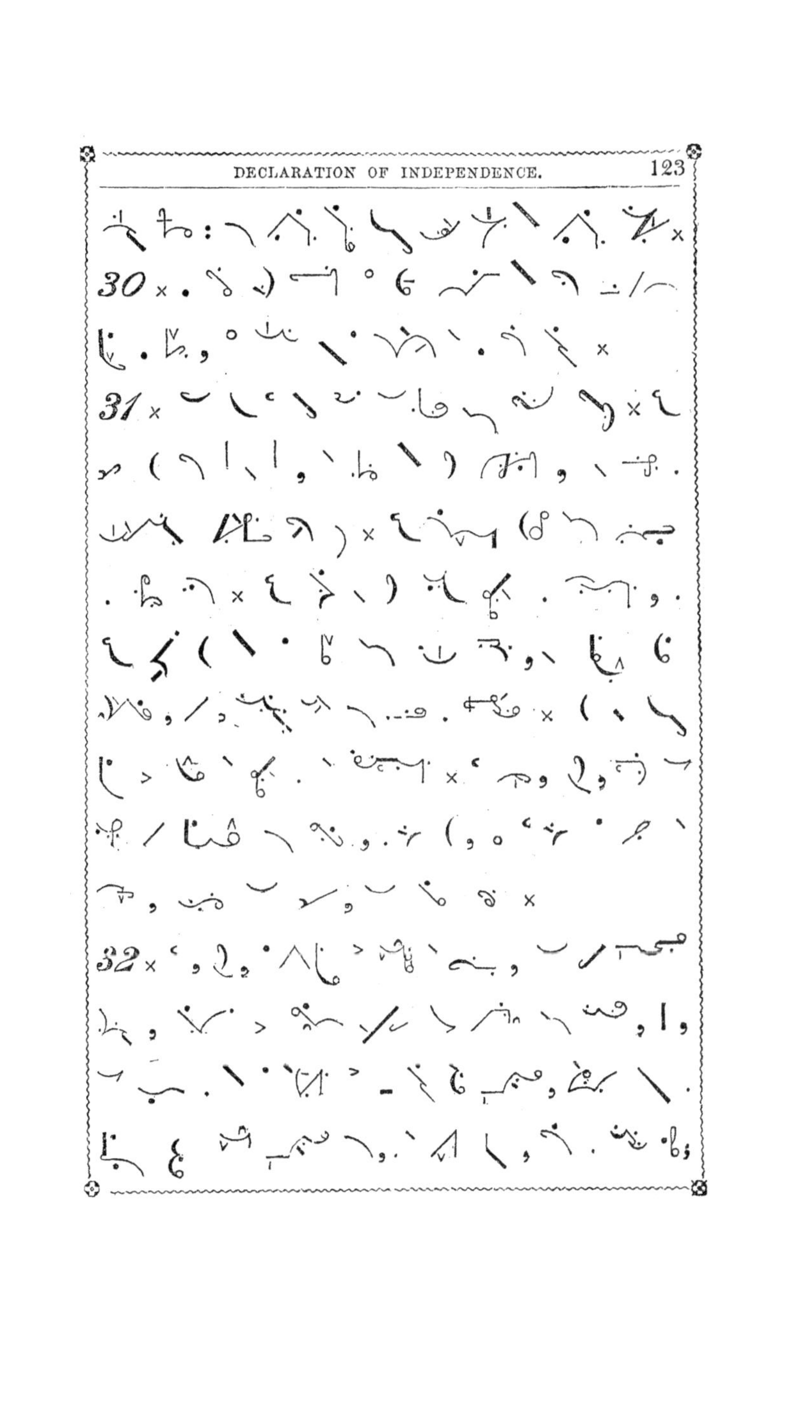
30
31
32

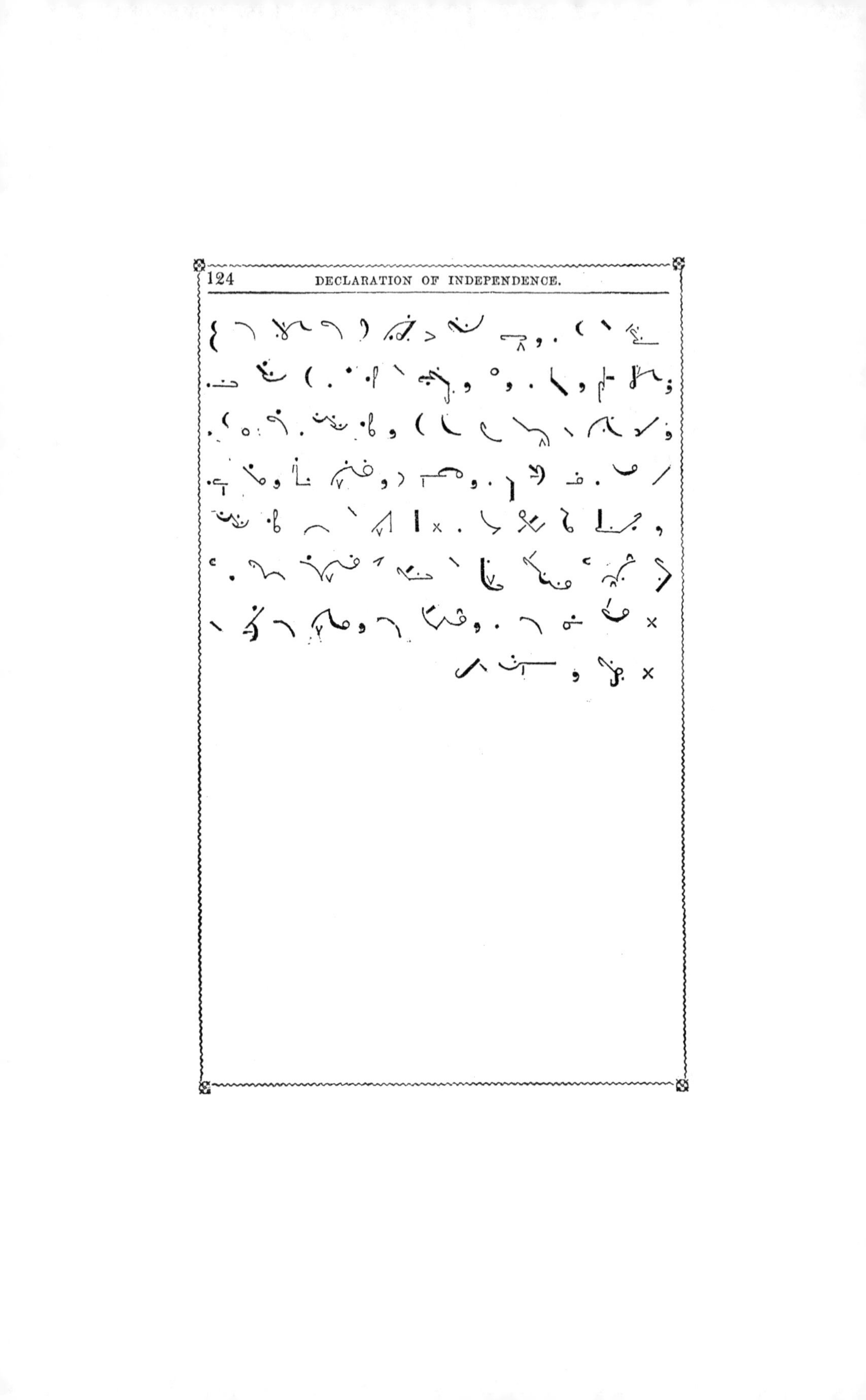

Opinions of Teachers

In regard to the Manual of Phonography.

The publishers of the MANUAL prefer giving the opinions of teachers who have used the book, and can speak from experience of its merits, to copying the editorial (and paid for) notices of reviewers who have most likely never read a dozen pages of the work, and know as little of Phonography itself. The expressions of approval below were entirely unsolicited, and of course were not designed for publication.

The first is from an experienced and competent Phonographic Teacher in Delaware (O.) College, H. PERSING.

I have seen Pitman's, Andrews and Boyle's, Webster's and Booth's text books on Phonography, and to all of these yours is far superior; the explanations being more lucid and the examples more copious than in any of the others; and indeed it is better calculated to give the private learner full instruction in the art than anything that has ever been presented to the public.

An excellent Phonographer, GEO. H. FLEMING, now in Buffalo, N Y., writes thus:

By the way, I like your Manual very much; I consider it as far ahead of Webster's, for real, practical instruction, as his work is in advance of Andrews & Boyle's Class-book. The rules for the upward R, L, and Σ, I consider invaluable; at least I know this, that if I had had them when I commenced the study of Phonography, it would have saved me easily one month's application, if not considerable more. The carrying out the phraseography to the extent you have, I think a very important and acceptable feature. The very limited extent to which this, and even the list of grammalogues are carried in the Class-book, was the cause of much dissatisfaction on my part toward that work, and when I obtained Webster's Teacher, his introducing a few new phrases and grammalogues was the cause of my preferring the Teacher to the Class-book; but on receiving the Manual, Teacher and Class-book were left, as our hoosier friends would say, "no whar."

"Please to send immediately two copies more of your Manual. I have just received those you sent me and of all the Phonographic instruction books that I have used, I think it is by far the best."—H. D. SMALLEY, New Baltimore, Ohio.

"I like your Manual better than anything I have yet seen." REV. J. W. TOWNER, Leroy, Ohio.

"The Manual has been received and is the best book of the kind I have seen. It is just the thing needed."—G. K. HICKOCK, Congress, Ohio.

A WORD OF ADVICE.

The student of Phonography, after he has gone through the MANUAL, will still need further help, to make him a fluent writer and ready reader. The author would suggest two sources from which to obtain aid: 1st. Membership in the AMERICAN PHONETIC SOCIETY; 2d, a subscription to the WEEKLY PHONETIC ADVOCATE and monthly shorthand SUPPLEMENT, advertisements of which see below.

THE AMERICAN PHONETIC SOCIETY.

This Society was established the first of November, 1848, having its origin in Cincinnati O. Its principal objects are,

1. The union and the co-operation of all friends of the Spelling Reform in the United States, Territories, and the Canadas.
2. To keep a census of the extent and progress of the reform movement.
3. And by publishing the names and addresses of new members every week in the *Phonetic Advocate*, and annually a list of the whole Society, to furnish each member with a directory that will enable him or her to hold correspondence, in phonetic writing, with individuals in almost any part of America,—thus rendering their phonetic knowledge of immediate practical advantage.

There are three classes of members: 1. Those who write phonetic shorthand: 2. Those who write only the phonetic longhand, whose names are printed in *italics;* and honorary members, distinguished by a * who contribute $1 or more to the Spelling Reform Fund. All other members are expected to contribute according to their ability and disposition to forward the great phonetic cause. Minors are requested to give their age.

The funds of the Society will be used to defray the expenses of publishing the Annual List, in printing tracts for gratuitous circulation, and other means of propagation.

Application for membership and contributions of money to be forwarded. post paid, to E. Longley, Secretary.

THE WEEKLY TYPE OF THE TIMES

Is a Journal of News, Science, Literature, Education and Reform.

Printed in Phonetic Spelling.

(*See Prospectus for* 1854 *on page*

SUPPLEMENT TO THE "TIMES."

16 PAGES, MONTHLY, AT 75 CTS A YEAR; OR 50 CTS WITH THE "TIMES."

The *Supplement* is the largest and cheapest Phonographic periodical published, either in this country or in England. It began its 3d volume in August, 1852, at which time the price was reduced one fourth. It is written in progressive styles of the art: the first half of the sheet in the simple Corresponding style, another portion in a kind of Transition hand, in which the reporting forms are explained by doted outlines, or the words re-written in long-hand; and a few pages, also, in the most condensed Reporting style. In the Corresponding style frequent suggestions will be given to assist the learner to an acquisition of a good style of writing, and the ability to read fluently; and from the English "Reporter," as well as from the best writers in our own country, will be presented such improvements in the Reporting style as may from time to time be made.

Thus the Supplement will constitute an invaluable companion to every phonographer in the United States, and it is hoped the low price at which it offered will secure for it a very large circulation.

www.ingramcontent.com/pod-product-compliance
Lightning Source LLC
LaVergne TN
LVHW021418110826
845150LV00007B/1985